Roland Schrapp

Astrological Studies on
Reincarnation, Death Horoscopes
and the Higher Essence of Rudolf Steiner

Roland Schrapp

Astrological Studies on Reincarnation, Death Horoscopes and the Higher Essence of Rudolf Steiner

English edition of the German book *Astrologische Betrachtungen zur Reinkarnation, zum Todeshoroskop und zur Wesenheit Rudolf Steiners*

Bibliographical information of the German National Library:
The German National Library lists this publication in the German National Bibliography. Detailed bibliographic data are available on the Internet at www.dnb.de.

Publisher: BoD · Books on Demand GmbH, In de Tarpen 42, 22848 Norderstedt, bod@bod.de
Print: Libri Plureos GmbH, Friedensallee 273, 22763 Hamburg

ISBN: 978-3-7693-2499-0

Contents

Preliminary Remarks

The horoscopes presented in this book were created using standard astrology software. These programs are uniformly based on the premise of traditional astrology, which assumes that the Sun is at 0° Aries at the start of spring. Yet, as Rudolf Steiner has shown, this was true only for a brief period of several decades before and after the year 1413, when the Age of Aries ended and the Age of Pisces began. Since then, the Sun's position at the start of spring has progressively shifted backward into the zodiacal sign of Pisces. This backward shift results from the slow retrograde motion of the Earth's axis, which moves approximately 1° every 72 years.

When creating horoscopes for individuals born in the centuries after 1413—including everyone alive today—the positions of both the planets and the house cusps must be adjusted several degrees backward. Cosmic conditions are not fixed; they are constantly in motion! The first degrees of a zodiac sign, as shown in the ephemerides, now actually belong to the preceding sign. Since 1413, the vernal equinox has shifted backward by 8.5°, nearly one-third of a zodiac sign. As a result, at the start of spring, the Sun no longer rises at 0° Aries, as stated in the ephemerides, but instead at 21.5° Pisces!

For a horoscope chart of someone born in the first half of this century, 8.5° must be subtracted from all planetary positions listed in the ephemerides to determine their actual positions. The same correction applies to the house cusps, especially the four cardinal points: Ascendant, Medium Coeli, Descendant, and Imum Coeli. A table of the necessary correction values has been provided by the author in his books *"Influences of the Forces of the Zodiac on the Cultural Development of Mankind"* and *"Ancient and Modern Worldview: Rudolf Steiner's Criticism of Astrology"*.

However, the astrological considerations in this book primarily focus on the "aspects" between the planets and their distances from the four main cusps of the chart. In this context, the exact positions within the zodiac signs are not crucial. For this reason, the enormous effort of extensive manual corrections in the horoscope charts has been omitted. It would not have provided any relevant additional insights.

Should We Take an Interest in Our Previous Incarnations?

In discussions among Anthroposophists on the subject of reincarnation, one occasionally encounters statements such as, "I don't engage with the question of who was who," or, "I'm not curious about who I was in a previous life." Such an attitude is undoubtedly a good safeguard against falling into illusions regarding one's former incarnations. However, it does not align with Rudolf Steiner's explicit wishes. He indeed considered it important that we take an interest in our previous incarnations.

Of course, this interest should never be driven by crude curiosity. Rudolf Steiner would undoubtedly have strongly advised against participating in so-called "regressions into previous earthly lives" conducted by other persons. Who could presume to grant others definitive access to one of their past incarnations? At best, such a feat would be possible only for a highly advanced initiate, and even such a person would rigorously reject such methods. What emerges in alleged regressions are typically unconscious desires and inclinations dwelling deep within the soul. These may sometimes relate to past incarnations, but such processes can never reliably determine a person's prior earthly life. Rudolf Steiner explicitly warned against such practices:

"It can't be denied from the outset that just in these things the worst foolishness is engaged in; many people have this or that experience and at once relate it to this or that former incarnation. [...]

But it should be clear that a spiritual investigator must have an eye for these things. It can really be so that something that happens to a person in childhood or youth returns to consciousness completely transformed in later life; then perhaps because the person does not recognize it, he takes it for a reminiscence from an earlier life on earth. [...]

One can also have an impression that whisks past so quickly that it does not come fully to consciousness and yet can return later as a distinct memory. A person—if he is not sufficiently critical—can then swear that this is something in his soul that was never experienced in his present life. It is thus understandable that such impressions cause all the foolishness in people who have busied themselves, but not seriously enough, with spiritual science.

This happens chiefly in the case of reincarnation, in which so much vanity and ambition is involved. For many people it is an alluring idea to have been Julius Caesar or Marie Antoinette in a former life. I can count as many as twenty-five or twenty-six Mary Magdalenes I have met in my lifetime! The spiritual investigator himself has good reason to draw attention to the mischief that can be stirred up in all this. [...]

What one was like in an earlier life is something we ordinarily cannot imagine, for it is usually just the opposite of what we might expect." [1]

Despite these warnings, Rudolf Steiner emphasized that engaging with reincarnation in a serious and objective manner is one of the core tasks of Anthroposophy. He explained:

---

[1] GA 147 "Geheimnisse der Schwelle" (Secrets of the Threshold), Munich, lecture of 27 August 1913

*"It means that just as an age was once ready to receive the Copernican theory of the universe, so is our own age ready for the ideas of **reincarnation and karma** to be brought into the general consciousness of humanity. And what is destined to happen in the course of evolution will happen, no matter what powers rise up against it. With the understanding of reincarnation and karma, all other insights will naturally follow. These insights flow from the light that emanates from the understanding of reincarnation and karma.*

*It is certainly useful to have considered the fundamental distinction between those who are interested in Anthroposophy and those who oppose it. The distinction does not really lie in the acceptance of a higher world, but in the way thoughts and conceptions change in the light of the **ideas of reincarnation and karma**. And so to-day we have been studying something that may be regarded as **the essence of the Anthroposophical world-view**."* [2]

In another lecture from the same year, Rudolf Steiner also emphasized:

*"But what is of prime importance is that those who profess to adhere to Anthroposophy as a cultural movement shall be so thoroughly steeped in the **ideas of reincarnation and karma** that they realise how life must inevitably become different if every human soul is conscious of these truths.*

The cultural life of the modern age has taken shape with the exclusion of consciousness of reincarnation and karma. And the all-important factor that will be introduced through Anthroposophy

[2]   GA 135 "Wiedergeburt und Karma und ihre Bedeutung für die Kultur der Gegenwart" (Reincarnation and Karma and their Significance in Modern Culture), Berlin, lecture of 5 March 1912

is that these truths will take real hold of life, that they will penetrate culture and in so doing essentially transform it." [3]

Since this is one of the primary missions of Anthroposophy, Rudolf Steiner attempted, from the very early years of his lecturing activity, to convey these ideas to his audience. In those days, he faced strong resistance. Later, he sought to foster an understanding of reincarnation and karma through artistic means, such as the Mystery Plays, the symbolic architecture of the first Goetheanum, and the weekly verses of the Anthroposophical Soul Calendar. [4]

Many of his listeners only began taking a serious interest in these topics after the devastating events of World War I, which claimed the lives of countless young people. This tragic loss kindled a broader interest in the afterlife and, by extension, in reincarnation and karma.

It was only after the Christmas Conference of 1923 that Rudolf Steiner dared to approach the subject in a concrete, cognitive manner. His lectures on "Karmic Relationships" of 1924, the year before his death, marked a decisive step:

"In this connection a new trend must take effect on our Movement, from now onwards. When the German Section of the Theosophical Society was founded in Berlin in 1902, I gave as the title of my first lecture: «Praktische Karmaübungen» (Practical Karma Exercises). The lecture was announced but could not be delivered for the simple reason that the prevailing conditions made

---

[3] GA 135 "Wiedergeburt und Karma und ihre Bedeutung für die Kultur der Gegenwart" (Reincarnation and Karma and their Significance in Modern Culture), Stuttgart, lecture of 21 February 1912

[4] See for example the author's book "The Anthroposophical Soul Calendar and the Incarnation Cycle of Man", Publisher BoD (Books on Demand), Norderstedt

it impossible. The older members of the Theosophical Society had their own ideas of what may or may not be spoken about, and this attitude had determined the whole atmosphere. The leading Members would have been horrified if at that time one had spoken of the practical Karma Exercises. The Theosophical Movement was not ready for it. A great deal of preparation was necessary and has, in fact, been going on now for more than two decades.

But at the Christmas Foundation Conference the impulse was given to reveal without reserve not only what can be researched about the natural realms of the spirit, but also what can be researched about the human realms of the spirit. And so in future we shall speak quite openly within the Anthroposophical Society of matters of which from the very beginning it was the intention to speak, but for which preparation had to be made. This is part of the esoteric trend and impulse with which the Anthroposophical Society was imbued through the Christmas Foundation Meeting." [5]

In his Karma Lectures of 1924, Rudolf Steiner fulfilled this intent in various ways. In a lecture the next day, for example, he explained how one can attain an understanding of the working of karma:

"For it is not in external similarities that we must seek for evidence of the working of karma; rather must we be observant of those things which in the deep foundations of a human being are carried over through karma from one earthly life into another. Perception of the karma of an individual human being, or even of one's own karma, requires the right attitude, the right mood-of soul. [...]

---

[5] GA 239 "Esoterische Betrachtungen karmischer Zusammenhänge – Band V" (Karmic Relationships V), Breslau (today Polish: Wrocław), lecture of 9 June 1924

*Every time you approach a karmic truth, you should actually feel something in your soul as if you were lifting a part of **the veil of Isis**. For in truth it is karma that reveals, in a way most intimately connected with human life, what Isis was—the Being designated outwardly as: «**I am that which was, is, and will be.**» This confronts us in a way that must touch the human soul when we consider human karma.*

In fact, it is only by contemplating, as we have just done, the unfolding of karma within the course of world history, and by thereby cultivating the necessary sacred mood for reflections on karma, that we can gaze with the proper attitude of soul upon our own karma, perceiving how it has unfolded and taken shape from earlier earthly lives through our experiences in the spiritual realms of the stars between death and rebirth. With our whole being we gaze at super-sensible worlds when we 'read' karma with the right mood-of-soul." [6]

As a significant guideline for exploring one's own past incarnations, Rudolf Steiner conveyed to his audience that people who belong to two entirely distinct karmic streams have come together in the Anthroposophical Society. It was his explicit wish that each individual reflect inwardly to discern to which of these streams they might belong. One stream began its incarnations on Earth at a very early stage, while the other only much later.

"The human souls came down at different times. There were those who descended comparatively soon, in the first periods of Atlantean development. But there were also those who came down relatively late—whose sojourn, so to speak, in the pre-earthly, planetary life was long. When we look back into the life of such a

---

[6] GA 239 "Esoterische Betrachtungen karmischer Zusammenhänge- Band V" (Karmic Relationships V), Breslau (today Polish: Wrocław), lecture of 10 June 1924

soul—beginning with the present incarnation—we come perhaps to a former Christian incarnation and maybe to yet another Christian incarnation. Then we come to the pre-Christian incarnations and so on. But we reach comparatively soon the earliest incarnation of such a soul, whereat we must say: Tracing the life still farther back from this point, it goes up into the planetary realms. Before this point, these souls were not yet present in earthly incarnations." [7]

Among the human souls who *"descended comparatively soon, in the first periods of Atlantean development,"* there were those who, within the Sun Oracle of ancient Atlantis, came to know Christ as the highest solar being. As a result, in their subsequent incarnations, *"their affiliation to **Christianity** was especially close to their hearts [...]. For this group, it is a profound solace that it can be unequivocally stated: the Anthroposophical Movement represents a movement that acknowledges and embodies the Christ impulse. Indeed, it would trouble their conscience if this were not the case."* [8]

In their first incarnations following the establishment of Christianity on Earth through the Mystery of Golgotha, these souls *"were still inspired by what lived in the ancient Greek Platonism. [...] It was **the Platonic stream**."* [9] Many of them reincarnated during the Middle Ages as Cistercians or within their sphere of influence.

The others, who began their incarnations on earth very late, were characterized by their much longer stay in the planetary spheres. In their earthly lives this was expressed in a great interest in the cosmos and the related teachings of the pre-

---

[7] GA 237 "Esoterische Betrachtungen karmischer Zusammenhänge – Band III" (Karmic Relationships III), Dornach, lecture of 8 July 1924

[8] Ibidem

[9] GA 240 "Esoterische Betrachtungen karmischer Zusammenhänge – Band VI", (Karmic Relationships VI), Arnheim, lecture of 18 July 1924

Christian mystery schools. Human souls of this kind find their access to anthroposophy primarily through the teachings on **cosmology**.

"Now as to the other group: In the manifestations of their life or in the manifestations of their personality, those who belong to it are indeed no less sincerely Christian. And yet, they come to Christianity from rather a different angle. This group initially finds fulfillment in the anthroposophical **cosmology**, *in the development of the Earth from other planetary forms, and in what Anthroposophy has to say about humanity in general. From this foundation, they are then naturally led toward Christianity."* [10]

After an incarnation in the final centuries before Christ, they ascended once more into the planetary spheres. At the time of the Mystery of Golgotha, they were in the sphere of the Sun, together with **Aristotle** and other significant individualities closely connected to the great Sun Archangel Michael. It was not until the early Middle Ages, from the 7th or 8th century AD onward, that they descended again for their next incarnation on Earth, and then once more in the centuries following the 13th century. Many incarnated at that time as Dominicans or in their immediate circles.

Rudolf Steiner's lectures on the karmic backgrounds of the Anthroposophical movement on earth were intended to inspire his listeners to engage with reincarnation in a concrete, not merely abstract, way. He therefore went on to reveal the earlier incarnations of a whole series of historical personalities and also their experiences in existence between two incarnations in the planetary spheres.

---

[10] GA 237 "Esoterische Betrachtungen karmischer Zusammenhänge – Band III" (Karmic Relationships III), Dornach, lecture of 8 July 1924

For some of these personalities, the date of their birth or at least their death has been handed down to us. This offers us the opportunity, to examine their horoscopes to see whether and, if so, in what way, prenatal experiences in the planetary spheres or even from previous incarnations can find expression in horoscopes. In this context, it is important to always take into account not only birth horoscopes but also death horoscopes. Rudolf Steiner also attached great importance to this.

Birth and Death Horoscopes

Modern astrology primarily concerns itself with natal horoscopes, which map the positions of the planets within the zodiac and houses at the moment of a person's birth. These positions are interpreted as the karmic foundation not only for the circumstances of this birth but for the entirety of the subsequent earthly life. According to Rudolf Steiner, however, the horoscope at the time of a person's death holds equally significant meaning, as death represents nothing less than a birth into higher spheres.

After shedding the physical body at death, the individual retains the etheric body as an external sheath for several days. The constellation of the planets at the moment of death is imprinted on this sheath like a mirror image. The imprint resonates within the individual, influencing his journey through the spheres and shaping his karma for the next incarnation. Steiner explains this as follows:

*"So in a most marked way do the forces of the starry constellations vibrate in the dead person who is still in his etheric body at the moment—which is, of course, karmically determined—when he has just left the physical world. Remarkable discoveries could be made if this process were approached with the necessary reverence and dignity—qualities often lacking even in the study of natal horoscopes, which are sometimes pursued for selfish reasons. Indeed, more selfless and profound results would emerge from examining the horoscope, in particular the **planetary** horoscope, **the positions of the planets** at the **moment of death**. This offers extraordinary revelations about the essence of the human soul and*

the intricate relationship between karma and the occurrence of death at a specific moment.

*Those who decide to conduct such investigations—the rules are the same as those applied to the birth horoscope—will make all kinds of interesting discoveries, especially if they were personally acquainted with the deceased during their lifetime. For several days the dead person bears within himself, in the etheric body he has not yet discarded, an echoing vibration of what comes from the **planetary** constellation. So the first phase is that of the direction in the starry constellation. It is meaningful as long as the human being remains connected with his etheric body."* [11]

The significance of the death horoscope extends even further. After spending, in most cases, centuries in the spiritual world, the individual returns to Earth, choosing a birth moment when the planetary alignments in the solar system closely resemble those at the time of their previous death.

"When a person passes through the gate of death he dies under a certain constellation of stars." By 'constellation of stars', Rudolf Steiner refers here specifically to the wandering stars, or planets, as becomes evident from the previous quote emphasizing the importance of the *"**planetary** horoscope"*, the *"**planetary** constellation"*, that is, the position of the planets in relation to each other, in the death horoscope. He then went on to talk about the significance of this constellation for the deceased:

"This constellation is significant for his further life of soul because it remains there as an imprint. In his soul there remains the endeavor to enter into this same constellation at a new birth, to do justice once again to the forces received at the moment of death. It is

---

[11] GA 174 "Zeitgeschichtliche Betrachtungen – Das Karma der Unwahrhaftigkeit – Teil 2" (Reflections on Contemporary History – The Karma of Untruthfulness – Part 2), Dornach, lecture of 21 January 1917

*an interesting point that if one tries to find out the star constellation of a human death, **the star constellation of the later birth coincides to a high degree with the star constellation of the previous death.** However, it must be remembered that the person is born at another spot on the earth that corresponds with this constellation. In fact, he is adapted to the cosmos, members himself into the cosmos, and thus a balance is established in the soul between the individual and the cosmic life."* [12]

Rudolf Steiner, through his spiritual research, has even revealed how the **planetary configurations** of a horoscope are formed:

*"Between death and rebirth our perfections and imperfections are faithfully recorded in the Akasha Chronicle. Certain attributes are inscribed in the Moon sphere, others in the Venus sphere, others in the Mars sphere, others in the Mercury sphere, others in the Jupiter sphere, and so on. **When we are returning to an incarnation** in a physical body and our being is slowly contracting, we encounter everything that was inscribed on the outward journey. In this way our karma is prepared. On the path of return we can **inscribe into our own being the record of our imperfections we ourselves first inscribed into the Akasha Chronicle**—not erase them, but embed them into our essence as a first step. They are not yet deleted.*

*Then we arrive on the earth. Because there is **within us** everything we inscribed into our being on the return journey, and we are obliged to inscribe a great deal even if not everything, because of this our karma unfolds. Up above, however, everything*

---

[12]   GA 140 "Okkulte Untersuchungen über das Leben zwischen Tod und neuer Geburt" (Occult Investigations on Life Between Death and Rebirth), Munich, first lecture of 26 November 1912

still remains inscribed. Now these inscriptions work together in a remarkable way. [...]

Then he comes back to the earth. He lives on the earth and has received into his karma what he has inscribed but at the same time it stands recorded above him." [13]

It is only through a new earthly life—and often through the course of several consecutive lives—that we gradually work through and erase the inscriptions of our imperfections from the various **planetary spheres**. This aligns perfectly with Steiner's earlier statement that *"in particular the **planetary** horoscope"*, the *"**planetary** constellation,"* is of great significance. The reason for this lies probably in the fact that the human soul processes the experiences of an earthly life primarily within the soul world, evolving karmically as a result.

According to Steiner, the soul world spans from the sphere of the Moon through those of Mercury and Venus to the Sun. It also permeates the three lower regions of the spiritual world, corresponding to the spheres Mars, Jupiter, and Saturn. The mobility of the planets and their orbital rhythms serve as a cosmic, symbolic reflection of the fluidity of the human soul, echoing Goethe's words: "Everything transitory is but a likeness."

When Steiner states, as quoted above, that ***"the star constellation of the later birth coincides to a high degree with the star constellation of the previous death,"*** it is important to note the phrase ***"to a high degree"***. This implies that the configurations are never entirely identical. One cannot expect the planetary positions of a death horoscope to be precisely replicated in the subsequent birth horoscope. Exact alignments of all

---

[13]   Ibidem, second lecture of 12 March 1913

planetary positions can only occur after tens of thousands of years.

Another critical factor must also be considered: our karmic connection with those individuals with whom we had close contact in our previous earthly life.

"Earthly life brings human beings together and what brings them together in life on earth also binds them karmically. They pass together through the life between death and rebirth. In cooperation with higher Beings they shape their karma for the next earthly life. What, then, is the consequence for a person's life on earth on the whole? On the whole, it follows that individuals who have been together in an earthly life where karma begins to form, will endeavour in the next earthly life to find their way to one another again. Once again they will establish karmic links, will again pass through the life between death and rebirth where a still stronger link is forged between them, and again seek for a common earthly existence. And here the remarkable fact comes to light that as Earth-evolution runs its course, human beings live together in groups.

If we look at this schematically, it is like this: time flows on; a certain group of human beings living as contemporaries in a particular epoch and karmically connected with one another, appears again on the Earth after the life spent between death and rebirth. A different group of human beings linked together by karmic ties appears on the Earth in a common existence; a third group likewise. As the periods between death and rebirth are by far the longer, it follows that the majority of human beings only meet in the life after death and before birth and that those specially connected with one another by karma pass through evolution in groups, coming together again and again on the Earth. That is the general rule. As a rule it is the case that on Earth we do not encounter those who formerly were not incarnated at the same time as ourselves." [14]

Each individual undergoes a highly unique post-mortem journey, often spending vastly different lengths of time in the various planetary spheres than we ourselves might experience. Furthermore, we each typically pass away at very different times and therefore under completely distinct planetary constellations. Nevertheless, individuals who are karmically closely connected tend to reincarnate as a group *in the same period of time*. This is only possible if there exists a certain 'range of alignment' in the planetary constellations of the death horoscopes and the subsequent birth horoscopes of these individuals.

Thus, Rudolf Steiner's statement about a 'high degree of coincidence' between death and birth horoscopes might be better understood in terms of a **'striking similarity'**, not so much in the positions of the planets within the zodiac signs, but rather in the **constellations formed by the planets in relation to one another**.

Such similarities seem to act as a 'red thread', a karmic thread, weaving one incarnation to the next and often linking a whole series of successive lives. This is because the resolution of our karma typically spans several lifetimes. Frequently, a life marked by significant developmental milestones is followed by one that is less momentous, serving more as a phase of retrospective internalization. As a result, the 'karmic thread' may often emerge even more clearly in the second subsequent incarnation than in the one immediately following.

---

[14] GA 239 "Esoterische Betrachtungen karmischer Zusammenhänge – Band V" (Karmic Relationships V), Breslau (today Polish: Wrocław), lecture of 11 June 1924

Indications in the Birth Horoscope of Pre-Birth Existence in Higher Realms

In some of his karma lectures delivered during the year before his death, Rudolf Steiner discussed specific examples illustrating how a person's pre-birth existence in the planetary spheres manifests in the planetary configurations of the next birth horoscope. Let us examine these examples in detail one by one.

Heinrich Heine

According to Rudolf Steiner, the German poet, writer, and journalist **Heinrich Heine**, after an incarnation as an Indian initiate roughly 2,000 years ago, underwent significant experiences in the spheres of **Mercury**, **Venus**, and **Mars**:

*"In comparatively early times, not long before the founding of Christianity, a certain Initiate was incarnated in the East, in the Indian civilisation. In his earthly life this individuality had poor eyesight—in describing karmic relationships one must go into details of this kind—and his perceptions remained more or less superficial. This life which was characterised by the mystical outlook typical of Indian culture, **was followed by other, less important incarnations.**"* [15]

---

[15] GA 239 "Esoterische Betrachtungen karmischer Zusammenhänge – Band V" (Karmic Relationships V), Breslau (today Polish: Wrocław), lecture of 9 June 1924

This example underscores that the resolution of our karma spans several incarnations. In Heine's case, too, significant aspects of his Indian incarnation during the early Christian era were not, or only partially, processed in at least two subsequent lives. Rudolf Steiner says clearly about Heinrich Heine's further development that his life in India was *"was followed by other, less important incarnations."* Thus, karma originating from a life as far back as the founding of Christianity—or even earlier—can still play out in our current earthly existence. In this sense, Rudolf Steiner elaborated further on Heine's developmental journey:

*"But there was a life between death and a new birth during which the superficial experiences of the Indian incarnation were worked upon in the Mercury sphere, partly too in the Venus sphere and in the Mars sphere, in conjunction with Beings of the higher Hierarchies. **In the majority** of human beings the influences of **one** of the cosmic spheres are **dominant** in the shaping of the karma."*

However, this was different with Heinrich Heine, as we have just learned: *"in the case of this particular individuality the influences of the **Mercury** sphere, the **Venus** sphere and the **Mars** sphere worked with almost equal strength at the karmic transformation of incipient faculties arising from the experiences of an Indian incarnation. In the nineteenth century this individuality appeared again as a somewhat complex personality, namely, **Heinrich Heine**. [...]*

*Life, even the life of an individual is certainly not impoverished but infinitely enriched in meaning when it is studied in the light of such foundations, when we can perceive the experiences of an earlier, Indian incarnation glimmering through that problematic, fragmentary Heine-life of the nineteenth century. Having absorbed the influences operating in the **Mercury** sphere and the **Venus** sphere, this individuality passed into the **Mars** sphere, where a certain strain of aggressiveness developed for the next earthly life;*

the experiences of an earlier life were transformed into a faculty in which there was a certain vein of aggressiveness. In the Mercury sphere the soul acquired the tendency to flit from one experience to another, one concept to another, and in the Venus sphere an element of eroticism—eroticism in the spiritual sense—crept into the imaginative, conceptual faculties."

Heinrich Heine was born on **December 13, 1797**, in Düsseldorf. If the birth time listed in the astro.com database —**3:20 p.m.**—is accurate, his natal horoscope would place Mercury, Venus, and Mars in prominent positions. These positions are defined as being near the four cardinal points (Ascendant, Medium Coeli, Descendant, and Imum Coeli) or in conjunction with one of the two 'lights,' namely the Sun or the Moon.

At the time of Heine's birth, **Mercury** was in conjunction with the **Sun** and additionally positioned at the Descendant. **Venus** was at the Midheaven, and **Mars** was in conjunction with the **Moon**.

It is probably such constellations in the horoscope that provide information about a person's prolonged prenatal presence in specific spheres: **conjunctions with the Sun and Moon**, and perhaps **oppositions** to them, as they are also highly significant aspects. Additionally, planetary positions **near the four major house cusps**, the cardinal points of the horoscope, hold great importance.

The zodiac signs in which the planets are located appear to play a lesser role. For example, **Mars** at Heine's birth might have been empowered by its placement in Scorpio, where it resided even after accounting for the precession of the equinoxes (approximately 5.5° for the late 1700s) [16]. Thus, Mars was situated at 2.5° Scorpio. However, the opposite was true for **Mercury**,

---

[16] See chapter "Preliminary Remarks"

which was in Sagittarius—a sign diametrically opposed to Gemini, the sign it governs. This placed Mercury in a weakened state, or 'exile.' Meanwhile, **Venus** was in the neutral environment of Aquarius.

It therefore seems that the positions of the planets in certain zodiacal signs are not really important here, in line with Rudolf Steiner's statement above, according to which *"in particular the **planetary** horoscope"* [17] is decisive. This principle provides a vital foundation for further analysis.

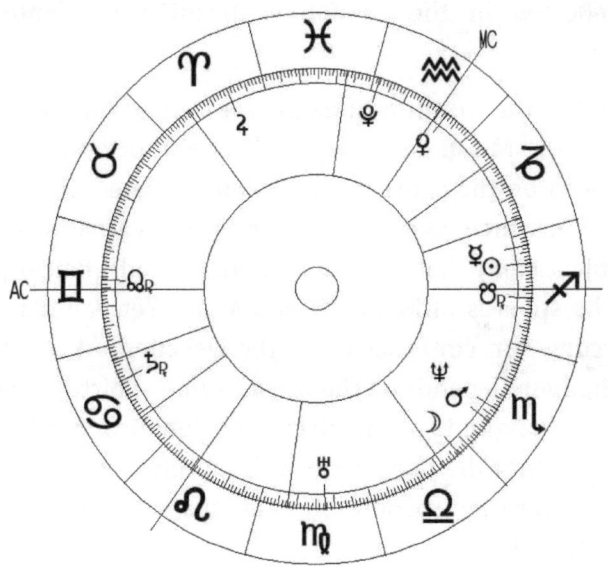

Heinrich Heine – Birth on December 13, 1797, at 3:20 p.m. (?)

---

[17]   See chapter "Birth and Death Horoscopes"

With regard to Heinrich Heine's distinctive pre-birth experiences in the **spheres of Mercury** and **Mars**, two **planetary groups** stand out in particular. First, the **conjunction** of **Mercury** with the **Sun** at the Descendant, and second, the **conjunction** of **Mars** with the **Moon**. The two "lights" (Sun and Moon) always hold special significance! The common restrictions on the orb of an aspect—limited to a few degrees for the planets and a maximum of 10 degrees for the Sun and Moon, as prescribed in many astrological teaching systems—do not apply here. As we shall see, the orbs must be considered much more broadly!

Heine's extended pre-birth sojourn in the **Venus sphere** is likely reflected in the prominent position of **Venus** at the **Midheaven**.

Naturally, the **conjunctions** of **Mercury** with the **Sun** and **Mars** with the **Moon** can also be observed in the horoscopes of anyone born on the same day as Heinrich Heine. However, each individual has their own unique series of incarnations. We may reasonably assume that all such individuals had a longer pre-birth stay in the spheres of **Mercury** and **Mars**. Yet, the placement of the **Mercury-Sun conjunction** at the **Descendant** and **Venus** at the **Midheaven** depends on the precise time of birth as well as the latitude and longitude of the birthplace. Identical positions at the angular points of the horoscope will, therefore, only occur in the charts of a very few people born on the same day as Heinrich Heine—perhaps even none of them.

Over the course of a lifetime, we all undergo further development. Nevertheless, certain fundamental traits of individuality persist across a series of successive incarnations. For this reason, it is worth examining Heinrich Heine's **death horoscope** to determine whether it reveals similar planetary constellations to those in his **birth chart**.

Heine passed away after a long illness at the age of 58 on **February 17, 1856**, in Paris. The exact time of his death is unknown. Consequently, his death horoscope was calculated for midday, at **12 noon**:

What immediately stands out is that at the time of Heinrich Heine's death, **Mercury** had moved even closer to the **Sun** than it had been at his birth. If his death occurred around midday, the Sun and Mercury would have occupied even a prominent position at the Medium Coeli, thereby gaining even greater emphasis. However, Mercury was only half a degree from the Sun. Such a close conjunction of Mercury with the Sun is often described in traditional astrology as a "combust Mercury" and typically interpreted negatively. Whether this traditional interpretation is correct, we leave open to question.

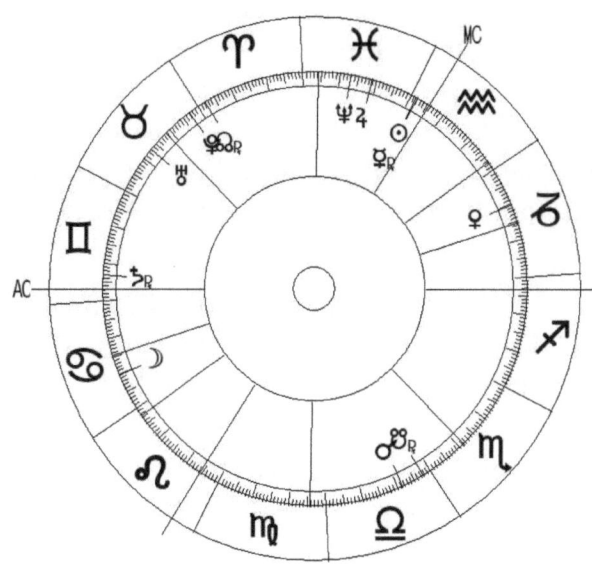

Heinrich Heine – Death on February 17, 1856 (12 noon ?)

In Heinrich Heine's **birth horoscope**, **Jupiter** was strikingly positioned in **opposition** to the **Moon**, while **Neptune** was in **conjunction** with **Mars**. At the time of his **death**, **Jupiter** and **Neptune** had joined the **Mercury-Sun conjunction**. This could suggest that, in the afterlife, the spheres of these two outer planets might have played a greater role. One might interpret this as a sign of Heinrich Heine's individual evolution.

In Heine's **birth horoscope**, **Venus** was 46° ahead of the **Sun**. As an "inner planet," Venus can only move up to 47° ahead of the Sun, a position known as "maximum *western* elongation." In his **death horoscope**, however, the situation was reversed. Venus was trailing the Sun, not at its maximum distance, but still 39° behind it—just 8° short of its "maximum *eastern* elongation." This, too, could be considered a notable feature.

Since the planets Mercury and Venus, due to their close proximity to the Sun, can never stand in opposition to it, one might ask whether their western and eastern elongations could be interpreted similarly to the oppositions of the "outer planets." If so, Venus would have held a "prominent" position in relation to the Sun at Heine's birth, solely due to this factor, regardless of its proximity to the Midheaven (assuming the recorded birth time is correct).

Had Heinrich Heine **passed away around 9 am**, **Venus** would once again have occupied a distinguished position at the Midheaven, similar to its position at his birth. **Mars**, which appeared in opposition to **Pluto** in the death horoscope, would then have gazed down from the Descendant, also from a prominent location. It must be noted, that the distances to the Midheaven remain speculative, as the exact time of Heine's death is unknown. However, we see **Mars** and **Pluto** in conjunction with the **lunar nodes**. As will become evident, this alignment also enhances the planets' significance!

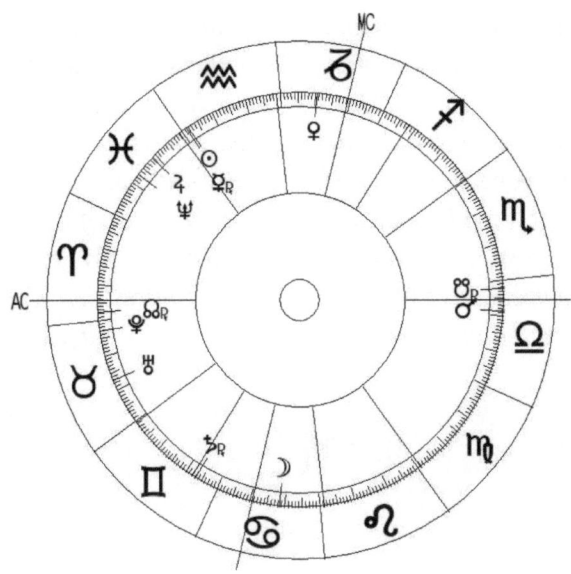

Heinrich Heine – Death around 9 a.m. ?

Voltaire

The French philosopher **Voltaire**, whose real name was **François-Marie Arouet**, was born on **November 21, 1694**, in Paris. Rudolf Steiner recounts an earlier incarnation of Voltaire in the 8th century CE, during the time when Islam expanded into Spain. According to Steiner, Voltaire first received an education in North Africa, influenced by Manichaean teachings. During this time, he became acquainted with remnants of the ancient mysteries, which were already in decline. Later, his path took him to Spain, where he encountered early Jewish Kabbalistic traditions. Both influences left a deep imprint on his soul.

*"This individuality then underwent further development during a life between death and rebirth, particularly in association with the beings connected to the **Mars region**. In this Mars existence, the individuality acquired a certain aggressiveness, as well as, alongside this aggressiveness, a linguistic agility—almost a seductive eloquence—that enabled it to address a wide range of issues with remarkable ease. These qualities were drawn from the soul's earlier earthly experiences. It was with these attributes that the individuality reincarnated in the eighteenth century, becoming **Voltaire**."* [18]

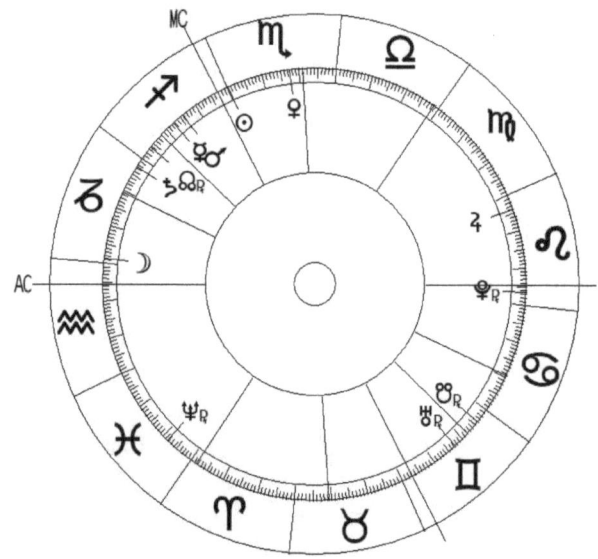

Voltaire – Birth on November 21, 1694 (12 noon ?)

Although Voltaire was born towards the end of the seventeenth century, in 1694, his earthly life extended well into the eighteenth

---

[18] GA 239 "Esoterische Betrachtungen karmischer Zusammenhänge – Band V" (Karmic Relationships V), Breslau (today Polish: Wrocław), lecture of 9 June 1924

century. He passed away in 1778. Thus, Steiner's reference to Voltaire's incarnation in the *"eighteenth century"* reflects the broader timeframe of his life. Unfortunately, as with Heinrich Heine, no precise birth time for Voltaire has been preserved. For the purposes of constructing the **natal horoscope**, midday —12 noon—was used as an approximate birth time.

Interestingly, **Mars**, representing the Mars sphere, was indeed in **conjunction** with **Mercury** near the **Sun** at the time of Voltaire's birth. If he was born around midday, this conjunction would have been located at the **Midheaven** (Medium Coeli). Even if he had been born at sunrise, sunset, or midnight, the planetary group would still have been prominently positioned at one of the horoscope's angular points. Accordingly, three alternative birth times produce the same notable emphasis on this planetary grouping.

Voltaire passed away on May 30, 1778, in his birthplace, Paris.

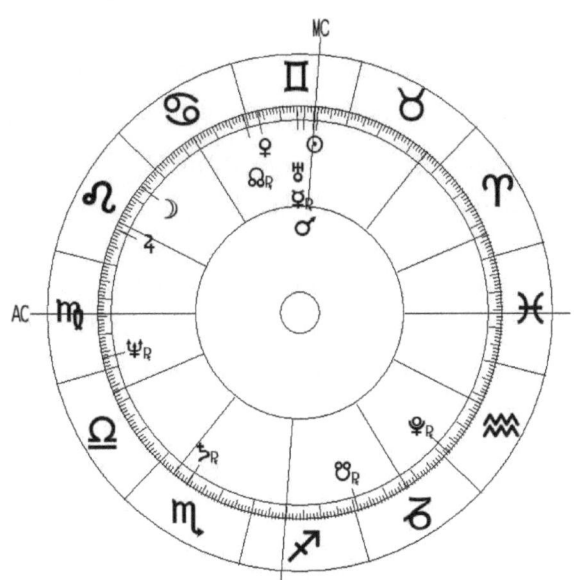

Voltaire – Death on May 30, 1778 (12 noon ?)

At the time of his **death, Mars, Mercury**, and the **Sun** had formed an even tighter **conjunction**, which was further joined by **Uranus** and **Venus**. If Voltaire died around noon, these planets would have also been located at the Midheaven. Another notable feature of his death chart is the **conjunction** of **Jupiter** with the **Moon**, potentially indicating an extended posthumous sojourn in the Jupiter sphere. The opposition of **Jupiter and Pluto** to the **Moon** at birth transformed into an opposition of **Pluto** to **Jupiter and the Moon**.

Goethe

The German poet, politician, and natural scientist **Johann Wolfgang Goethe**—ennobled in 1782 as "von Goethe"—was, according to his own account in *Dichtung und Wahrheit* (Poetry and Truth, Part 1, Book 1), born *"on **August 28, 1749, at noon**, precisely as the clock struck twelve,"* in Frankfurt am Main. Rudolf Steiner described a prolonged sojourn in the **Jupiter sphere** as preceding Goethe's incarnation in the 18th/19th century:

"There is an individuality who leads us back to ancient Greece, into a milieu of Platonism, and also of sculpture. This individuality had a very significant incarnation as a sculptor in Greece. What he there experienced was carried over into intermediate incarnations of less importance. This is an individuality whose karma for what is at the moment his latest incarnation was elaborated chiefly in the sphere of Jupiter's wisdom." [19]

As with Heinrich Heine, Goethe's most recent incarnation also reflected karma rooted in a third-prior incarnation. Steiner noted

---

[19]   GA 239 "Esoterische Betrachtungen karmischer Zusammenhänge – Band V" (Karmic Relationships V), Breslau (today Polish: Wrocław), lecture of 9 June 1924

that Goethe carried those experiences into later *"intermediate incarnations"* that were *"of less importance."* In the same lecture, Steiner specified that Goethe's *"life as a man in Greece was followed by female incarnations."*

Steiner often referred to *"less significant incarnations"* in his karma lectures. These appear, in many cases, to have been female incarnations, where historical circumstances offered fewer opportunities to develop into prominent figures due to the patriarchal systems that dominated the last few millennia. Rare exceptions, such as the mathematician Hypatia of Alexandria in the 4th century CE or the German nun Roswitha of Gandersheim in the 10th century, demonstrate that significant female incarnations were possible, though uncommon. In most cases, however, our female incarnations seem to have served primarily for internalization and soul-deepening. With the growing equality of the sexes and the increasing public roles of women—ranging from leadership positions to governance—more female incarnations will undoubtedly be counted among the historically significant lives of humanity henceforth.

Returning to Goethe, Rudolf Steiner's statement about a prolonged prebirth sojourn in the **Jupiter sphere** aligns intriguingly with Goethe's birth chart. His horoscope shows a close **conjunction** of **Jupiter** with the **Moon**, one of the two "lights" that always enhance the significance of associated planets. Moreover, this **conjunction** is positioned near the **Imum Coeli** and gains additional emphasis through its **opposition** to the **Sun** at the **Medium Coeli**. The **Sun**, in turn, is **conjunct Mercury**. In the **Mercury sphere** after death, humans learn to perceive that the sensory world's maya is based on a higher, supersensory reality. This was Goethe's fundamental conviction, expanded and significantly deepened by his prenatal experiences in the wisdom sphere of **Jupiter**.

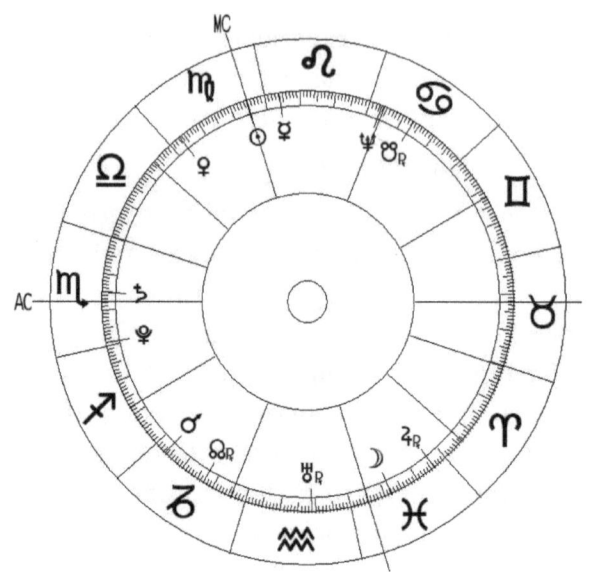

Goethe – Birth on August 28, 1749 at 12 noon

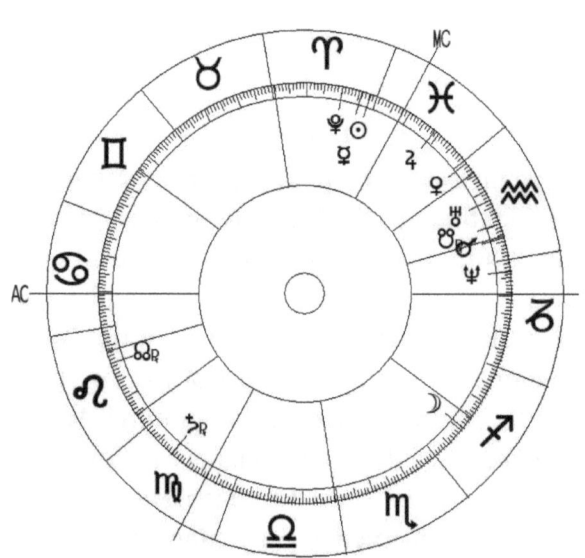

Goethe – Death on March 22, 1832 around 11:30 a.m.

According to family accounts, Goethe passed away in Weimar in the late morning of **March 22, 1832**, around **11:30 a.m**. His **death chart** once again reveals the **Sun-Mercury conjunction** at the **MC**. By this time, **Jupiter** and **Pluto** had joined this grouping, suggesting another significant post-death sojourn in the Jupiter sphere, as well as encounters in an even higher cosmic realm.

The exact **opposition** of **Saturn** to **Jupiter** and to the **Sun** in Goethe's **death chart**, positioned near the **Imum** and **Medium Coeli**, hints at an additional prolonged post-death experience in the **Saturn sphere**. Conjunctions and oppositions both appear to play a significant role in this context.

Éliphas Lévi

The writer and occultist **Éliphas Lévi Zahed**, born **Alphonse Louis Constant**, was born on **February 8, 1810**, in Paris. According to Rudolf Steiner, his birth was preceded by an extended post-mortem sojourn in the **Jupiter sphere**, similar to Goethe, yet distinctly different in nature, reflecting the profound differences between their individualities. Before the (re)discovery of America by Columbus, Éliphas Lévi had been incarnated in Mexico as a participant in the then-declining mysteries of Quetzalcoatl. Following that life, he experienced no further "less significant incarnation" and was reborn in the 19th century as a man.

Steiner explains that Éliphas Lévi *"also passed through the* ***Jupiter sphere****, where his experiences in the Mexican Mysteries were cast into a new form. But the Jupiter sphere could not produce identical results from an earthly life in Greece [Goethe] and an earthly life in Mexico of the kinds I have described. Both sets of experience were worked upon by the wisdom of the Jupiter sphere* *but both were conditioned by the formative forces that had been in operation in earlier lives.*

The individuality who had been connected with the Mexican Mysteries lived through the Jupiter sphere and was reborn as Éliphas Lévi. There you have an example of how magic practices, magic rites and enactments have been transformed in a remarkable way into wisdom. It is Jupiter-karma of an inferior kind, but for all that replete with spirituality, replete with wisdom. From this we perceive how what a man has experienced in earthly life works into what he becomes during his life between death and a new birth. The later life is invariably conditioned by the earlier life. But the experiences of earthly life can be transformed by the selfsame sphere into very different karma. Our view of human life can only be deepened in the right way when we perceive how this life is shaped in conformity with karma. Then it is enriched, then and only then do we acquire a real knowledge of man and of human life." [20]

Éliphas Lévi passed away on May 31, 1875, in his birthplace of Paris. The exact time of his death is unknown, so the **death horoscope** below illustrates the celestial configuration at noon. A striking feature of his **birth chart**—the near-exact **conjunction** of the **Moon**, **Jupiter**, and the **descending lunar node**—appears in a transformed state in the **death horoscope**. Here, the **Moon** has joined the **ascending lunar node** and stands in near-exact **opposition** to **Jupiter**, which is again positioned at the **descending lunar node**. This can likely be interpreted as a sign of another prolonged post-mortem sojourn in the **Jupiter sphere**, though certainly at a higher level of development. Furthermore, this highlights once again the significant role of conjunctions and oppositions in such contexts.

---

[20] GA 239 "Esoterische Betrachtungen karmischer Zusammenhänge – Band V" (Karmic Relationships V), Breslau (today Polish: Wrocław), lecture of 9 June 1924

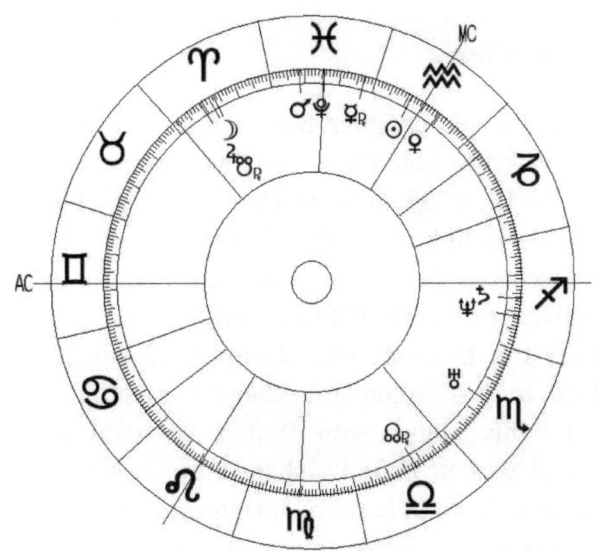

Éliphas Lévi – Birth on February 8, 1810 (12 noon ?)

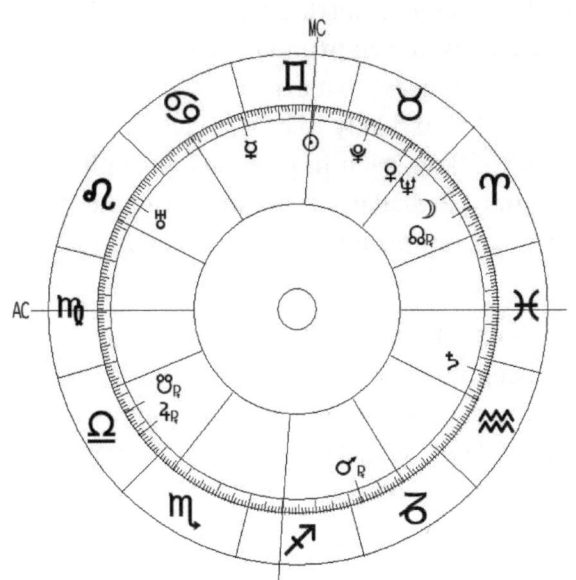

Éliphas Lévi – Death on May 31, 1875 (12 noon ?)

Friedrich Schiller

The German poet, philosopher, historian, and physician **Friedrich Schiller**, elevated to nobility in 1802 as "von Schiller," was **born on November 10, 1759**, in Marbach am Neckar. The exact time of his birth remains unknown, though some biographical accounts suggest it occurred between 10 and 11 PM. For the following chart, a birth time of 11:30 PM has been assumed, as this positions **Saturn** near the **Descendant**, placing it in **opposition** to the **Moon** close to the Ascendant, thereby further enhancing its significance. This aligns with Rudolf Steiner's assertion that Schiller's soul was profoundly shaped by an extended prenatal sojourn in the **sphere of Saturn**, during which he worked through deeply stirring experiences stemming from a previous incarnation during the brutal persecutions of Christians in the 1st and 2nd centuries AD. [21]

Additionally, Schiller's birth chart reveals **Mercury** near the **Sun**, as well as **Mars** and **Neptune** in close proximity to the **Moon**. These placements suggest that experiences in the spheres associated with these planets likely played a significant role in shaping his karma. As we have seen in previous examples, **conjunctions** and **oppositions**, particularly those involving the "lights" **Sun** and **Moon**, hold great importance in reincarnative interpretations of horoscopes.

At Schiller's **death** on **May 9, 1805**, **Saturn** and **Uranus**, which had already been in close proximity at his birth, had drawn even nearer, forming a **conjunction** with the **Moon** instead of **Mars** and **Neptune**. This suggests another prolonged posthumous sojourn in the **Saturn sphere** for Schiller.

---

[21] GA 239 "Esoterische Betrachtungen karmischer Zusammenhänge – Band V" (Karmic Relationships V), Breslau (today Polish: Wrocław), lecture of 10 June 1924

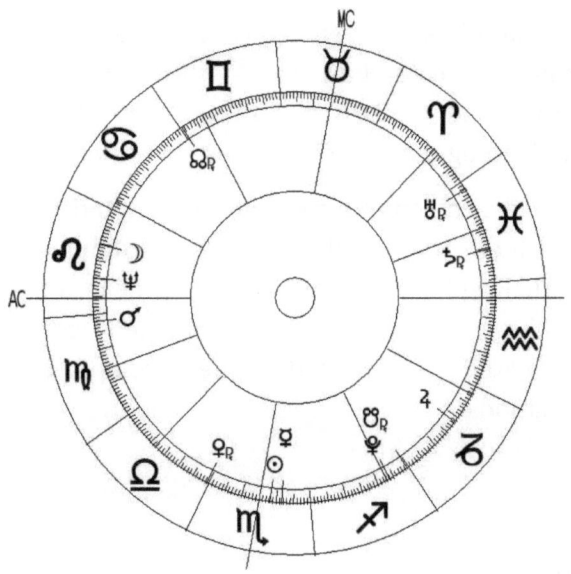

Friedrich Schiller – Birth on November 10, 1759 (11:30 p.m. ?)

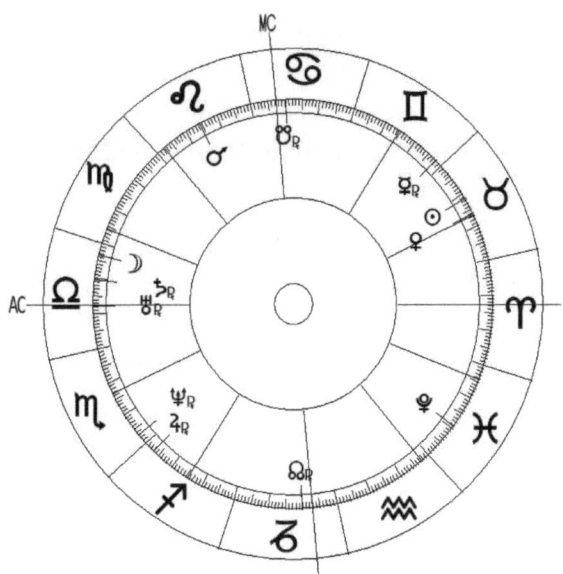

Friedrich Schiller – Death on May 9, 1805 around 4:30 p.m.

Schiller's death is believed to have occurred **between 4 and 5 PM**, and thus his death chart was cast for 4:30 PM. This timing positions the triad of **Saturn**, **Uranus**, and the **Moon** at the **Ascendant**, lending these celestial bodies additional emphasis.

Moreover, a close **conjunction** of the **Sun** and **Venus** appears in this chart, indicating the likelihood of an extended posthumous sojourn in their spheres as well. While we generally traverse all planetary spheres after death, the duration and significance of our experiences within each depend on the development achieved in prior incarnations.

Victor Hugo

The renowned French writer and politician **Victor-Marie Hugo** was **born on February 26, 1802**, at **10:30 PM** in Besançon. His birth time is historically documented. According to Rudolf Steiner, Hugo's incarnation in the 19th century was preceded by a life as a woman, about which Steiner provides no further details. Prior to that, Victor Hugo lived as a man in Ireland and was initiated into the Hibernian Mysteries:

"There is an individuality who in very early times had attained a certain degree of Initiation in the Hibernian Mysteries and then, later on, passed through a female incarnation—but the influence of the Hibernian incarnation worked deeply, very deeply upon the soul. Then, in a life between death and a new birth, this individuality lived through experiences arising when karma is wrought out in the ***Saturn sphere.*** *The whole significance of what the soul had acquired in an Hibernian Initiation—not at the highest but at a certain stage—was seen in retrospect, in a perspective widening out into a vista of great cosmic happenings. The import of the*

knowledge which it was possible to acquire in Hibernia was seen in its relation to the whole past evolution of man." [22]

How much of the magnificence of such an incarnation as an initiate of the Hibernian Mysteries—and the subsequent Saturn sphere processing—can be brought into the next earthly life depends significantly on the nature of the physical body available in the new incarnation. Steiner elaborates:

"However, because this [magnificent prebirth experience] *had to submerge into a body not akin to the remarkable bodies of the ancient Irish initiates but rather to that of a 19th-century French-man, much of it receded into the background, transforming itself into sublime but fantastic pictures which, however have a certain power, a certain grandeur about them. This individuality reincarnated as* **Victor Hugo**. *There again we can perceive how karma works on, even when two incarnations differ as greatly as do the lives of the Irish Initiate and Victor Hugo. For it is not in external similarities that we must seek for evidence of the working of karma; rather must we be observant of those things which in the deep foundations of a human being are carried over through karma from one earthly life into another."*

Given Victor Hugo's significant prebirth experience in the **Saturn sphere**, it is reasonable to expect that **Saturn** would hold a prominent position in his birth chart, through conjunction or opposition with the Sun or Moon or proximity to one of the chart's angular points.

Indeed, in Hugo's horoscope, **Saturn** is found conjunct **Jupiter** near the **Midheaven** and in an almost exact **opposition** to the **Sun**, which appears close to **Pluto** and **Venus**.

---

[22] GA 239 "Esoterische Betrachtungen karmischer Zusammenhänge – Band V" (Karmic Relationships V), Breslau (today Polish: Wrocław), lecture of 10 June 1924

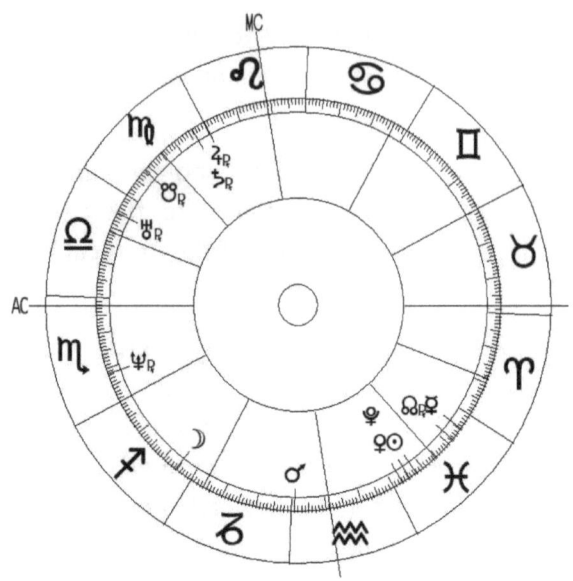

Victor Hugo – Birth on February 26, 1802 at 10:30 p.m.

It is worth examining whether this planetary configuration is at least partially reflected in Hugo's **death horoscope**, as an indicator of his individuality.

Victor Hugo **died** on **May 22, 1885**, in Paris. Since the exact time of death is unknown, the death chart was cast for noon. In this speculative chart, the **Sun** is positioned at the **Midheaven**. Remarkably, after 83 years, the **Sun** again appears in close **conjunction** with **Pluto** and **Venus**, underscoring Hugo's individuality.

Interestingly, this case demonstrates not only connections between the death horoscope of a previous life and the birth chart of the subsequent incarnation but also parallels between the birth and death charts of the same earthly life.

Another such similarity can be observed with the planet **Mercury**. At Hugo's death, Mercury was positioned at a similar distance from the **Sun** as at his birth, but now joined by **Neptune** and **Mars**. At birth already, the latter was on the same side of the horoscope as the **Sun**, **Pluto**, **Venus** and **Mercury**. Finally, **Saturn** joined this large group.

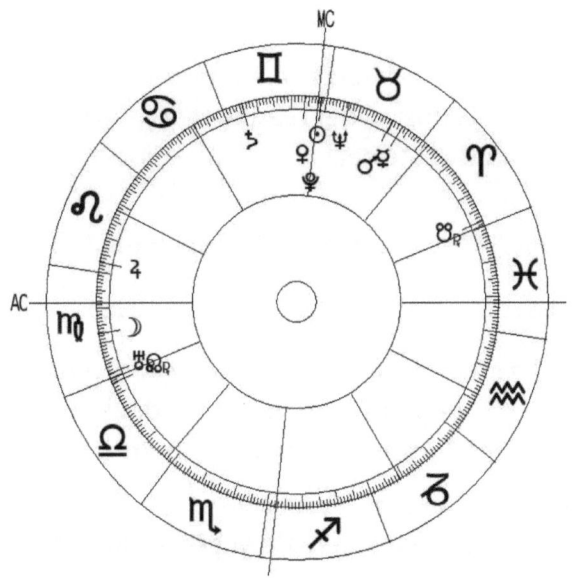

Victor Hugo – Death on May 22, 1885 (12 noon ?)

Jupiter, which was in **opposition** to the **Sun** in Hugo's **birth chart**, appears near the **Moon** and **Uranus** at the time of his **death**, forming a wide **conjunction** with them.

Notably, the planets in Hugo's charts tend to cluster around one of the two "lights". Even the ascending lunar node was close to the Moon at the time of his death.

45

Successive Incarnations

Important note!

The following section presents comparative analyses of the horoscopes of several historical figures and their previous incarnations as revealed by Rudolf Steiner.

It is ESSENTIAL to observe the following PRINCIPLE:

Striking astrological similarities between the horoscopes of successive incarnations of an individual may serve as a confirmation of Rudolf Steiner's statements.

HOWEVER: The actual occurrence of reincarnation can NEVER (!!!) be proven solely through astrological means!

If someone discovers similarities between their own horoscope and that of a historical figure, they cannot conclusively infer a reincarnational connection to that person. Every day, numerous individuals are born under the same planetary alignments, some even at nearly the same time and in close geographic proximity, resulting in ascendants and other house cusps in their horoscopes that may not differ significantly.

Similarly, on the day a historical figure was born, other individuals were also born simultaneously or very close in time, and sometimes even in the same vicinity. Moreover, the death and subsequent birth horoscopes being compared will never completely match. At most, they may exhibit partial resemblances. Even if these similarities appear astonishing in some cases, the occurrence of reincarnation can never be definitively proven by astrological analysis alone!

With this crucial principle in mind, the death and subsequent birth horoscopes of historical figures will now be compared, relying on Rudolf Steiner's explicit assurance that, according to his spiritual-scientific research, these cases represent actual reincarnations.

Pope Gregory VII (Hildebrand) – Ernst Haeckel

Between 1025 and 1030, the monk **Hildebrand** was born. The exact date remains unknown, making it impossible to construct a birth horoscope. In 1073, Hildebrand was elected as **Pope Gregory VII** of Rome and became known for initiating the Gregorian Church reforms of the 11th century. He **passed away** on **May 25, 1085**, in Salerno. Based on this date, a **death horoscope** can at least be approximated.

According to Rudolf Steiner, the post-mortal passage through the **Saturn sphere** was formative for this individuality. We may therefore reasonably assume an emphasis on **Saturn** in Gregory VII's **death horoscope**. However, whether Saturn is close enough to the Sun and Moon to establish such an emphasis remains questionable. Assuming Saturn might have occupied a critical position in the horoscope, a speculative time of 2:15 a.m. was chosen as the death moment. This would place **Saturn**, along with **Venus**, rising in the east at the Ascendant. However, other angular positions could also be plausible.

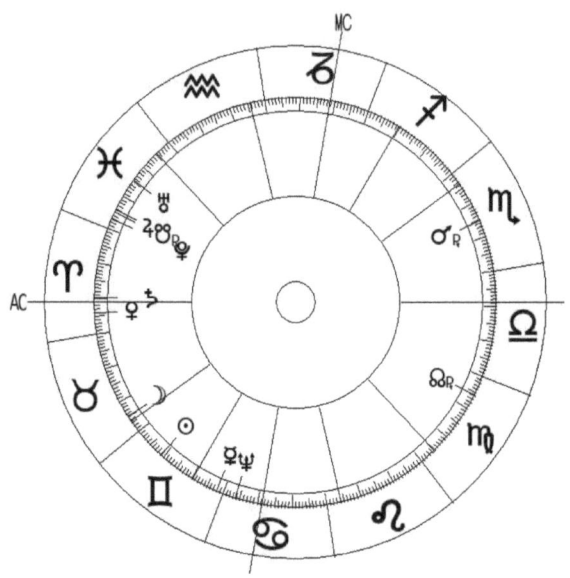

Papst Gregory VII – Death on May 25, 1085 (2:15 a.m. ?)

The individuality of Pope Gregory VII was reborn in the 19th century as the German physician, zoologist, and philosopher **Ernst Haeckel**. Rudolf Steiner referred to Haeckel's *"most important previous earthly incarnation as Pope Gregory [...], who had come as Hildebrand from the Cluniac reforms."* [23]

---

[23] GA 239 "Esoterische Betrachtungen karmischer Zusammenhänge – Band V" (Karmic Relationships V), Breslau (today Polish: Wrocław), lecture of 10 June 1924

This example shows that the same individuality can hold vastly different views in successive earthly lives, even to the point of embodying outright contradictions. So here we encounter the *"fact that Ernst Haeckel, who fought the church so furiously, was the reborn monk Hildebrand, who was the great pope Gregory in his previous incarnation. From this, we see how insignificant the external content of a person's beliefs or views is in earthly life, as these are merely their thoughts. However, study Haeckel, and particularly Gregory in connection with his role as Abbot Hildebrand, and you will perceive a dynamic continuity at work."*

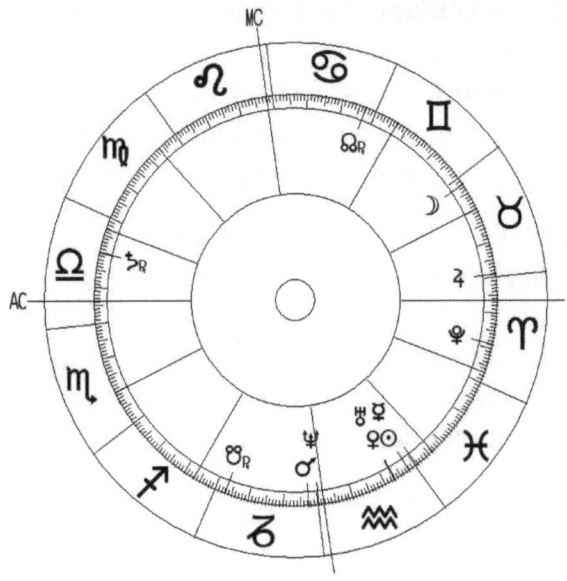

Ernst Haeckel – Birth on February 16, 1834 at 10:30 p.m. (?)

Ernst Haeckel was born on **February 16, 1834**, in Potsdam. Astro-seek.com lists his **birth time** as **10:30 p.m.**, albeit without citation. If accurate, **Saturn** would have been prominently positioned near the Ascendant, aligning with Steiner's assertions that Haeckel developed his karma during an extended sojourn in the **Saturn region**.

At first glance, the **death horoscope of Gregory VII** seems vastly different from **Haeckel's birth horoscope**. However, closer analysis reveals striking similarities, particularly involving the **outer planets**. In both horoscopes, **Neptune** is located near the **Sun**, forming a wide **conjunction**.

Additionally, **Jupiter** and **Pluto**, which were tightly **conjunct** at **Gregory VII's death**, are also adjacent in **Haeckel's birth chart**, albeit in a looser **conjunction**. Taking into account the precession of the vernal equinox due to the slow rotation of the Earth's axis, **Jupiter** was in **Aries**, that is, in the same sign as **Pluto**, because in 1834 the zodiac sign Aries actually only ended at 6° Taurus. See the "Preliminary Remarks" at the beginning of this book.

At **Haeckel's birth**, **Pluto** was also in an almost exact opposition to **Saturn**, further emphasizing this planet positioned at the Ascendant, which represents Haeckel's significant pre-birth experiences in the Saturn sphere. Once again, we see that, beyond planetary positions at the angular points of a horoscope, **oppositions** and **conjunctions** are of particular importance.

Venus, which was in **conjunction** with the significant **Saturn** at the time of **Gregory VII's death**, and **Uranus**, which was near the **Jupiter-Pluto conjunction**, came together in Haeckel's reincarnation to form a **conjunction** with the important **Sun**, accompanied by **Mercury**. In addition, at **Haeckel's birth**, the **Moon** was in almost the same position as in **Pope Gregory's death chart**.

The two horoscopes, which initially appear so dissimilar, actually reveal a number of similarities that can certainly be seen as an astrological confirmation of Rudolf Steiner's statement that this is a case of reincarnation.

What did **Ernst Haeckel's death horoscope** look like? Does a 'red thread' of continuity weave through his incarnations? Did the astrological links to his prior life as Gregory VII persist until his next death on earth? **Ernst Haeckel** died on **August 9, 1919**, in Jena, but the exact time is unknown. His **death horoscope** was speculatively set for noon.

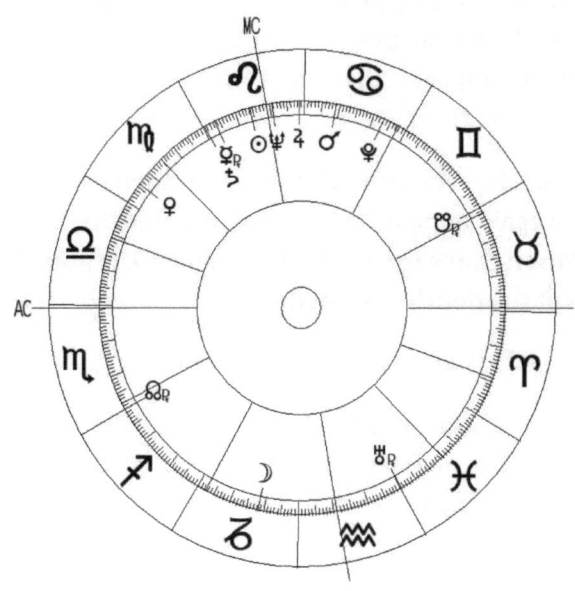

Ernst Haeckel – Death on August 9, 1919 (12 noon ?)

It immediately stands out that **Jupiter** and **Pluto**, which already played a significant role in **Gregory VII's death horoscope** due to their very close conjunction, are now positioned **near the Sun**, thereby amplifying their influence. **Mars** and **Neptune** have joined them at the time of **Ernst Haeckel's death**. These two planets were already in **conjunction** in **Haeckel's birth horoscope**.

Furthermore, we see the important **Saturn** close to the **Sun**, now in close conjunction with **Mercury**, which was already near the Sun at the time of Haeckel's birth—a position that is not unusual for Mercury. The tight **conjunction** between **Mercury** and **Uranus** that existed at the time of his birth has now shifted into an equally close **opposition** at the time of his death. Once again, this underscores the great significance of conjunctions and oppositions. It appears that they can even alternate between successive incarnations.

Venus, in close **conjunction** with **Saturn** at **Gregory VII's death**, once again appears near **Saturn** in **Haeckel's death chart**. Even the **Moon-Mars opposition** present at **Gregory VII's death** reemerges at the **death of Haeckel**.

Taken together, these findings are astonishing.

However, the positioning of the major planetary grouping at the Medium Coeli in Haeckel's death chart is contingent on the speculative assumption of a noon death time.

Cardinal Mazarin – Count Georg von Hertling

The French cardinal and statesman **Jules Mazarin** was born on **July 14, 1602**, in Pescina, in the Kingdom of Naples. His horoscope is listed on astro.com with a **birth time of 7:05 PM**, though without a specific source. This raises doubts about the accuracy of the stated time. Therefore, we will focus solely on analyzing the planetary configurations.

Cardinal Mazarin experienced a previous incarnation—likely his penultimate—toward the end of the 1st century AD. According to Rudolf Steiner, he was *"a philosopher, most evidently one of the Sceptics, that is to say, he was one of those **who really think nothing in the world is certain**. He belonged to that sceptical School which though it already saw the dawn of Christianity, stood altogether on the ground **that it is impossible to gain certain knowledge**, and above all that it is quite impossible to say with certainty whether a Divine Being could assume a human form or the like."* [24]

This nebulous attitude of "holding nothing as certain" bears an astrological resemblance to the influence of **Neptune**. Nonetheless, Steiner informs us: *"We see him, elaborating his karma most especially in the region of Mercury, so that he is able to see many things, not in an inward sense but in the sense of being gifted with outward intelligence. He gains a wide sweep of vision for many facts and relationships. As we follow this individuality further, we find him again on earth. We find him as the Cardinal who carried on the Government of Louis XIV when Louis XIV was still a child: **Cardinal Mazarin.**"*

---

[24] GA 238 "Esoterische Betrachtungen karmischer Zusammenhänge – Band IV" (Karmic Relationships IV), Dornach, lecture of 19 September 1924

Mercury, the physical representative of the supersensible **Mercury sphere**, can never move far away from the Sun due to the proximity of its orbit to the Sun. It is therefore possible that its maximum western and eastern elongations should be regarded similarly to oppositions and considered as emphasized positions. Whether Mercury at Mazarin's birth was also near the Descendant or one of the other three angular points of the horoscope cannot be definitively determined due to the uncertain birth time. If the reported time of 7:05 PM is accurate, **Mercury**, along with **Venus** and the **Sun**, was positioned in the west, thereby gaining additional prominence.

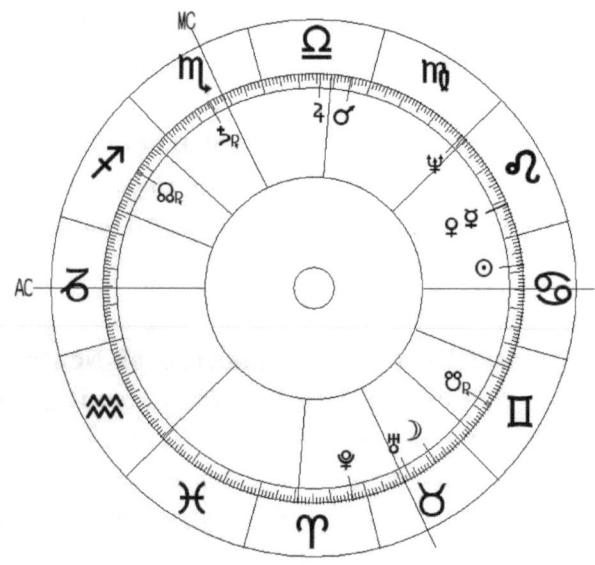

Jules Mazarin – Birth on July 14, 1602 (7:05 p.m. ?)

Notably, **Neptune** is located near **Mercury**, and we might even consider the planets **Neptune**, **Mercury**, **Venus**, and the **Sun** as forming a **conjunction group**. This grouping could reveal the 'red thread' of this individuality, weaving through multiple incarnations.

When analyzing horoscopes from a reincarnational perspective, conjunctions and oppositions may need to be interpreted more broadly than traditional astrology suggests. It may suffice for planets to occupy the same quadrant or stand in opposition to the opposite quadrant. If so, the planetary grouping of **Saturn, Jupiter** and **Mars, opposing Pluto, Uranus** and the significant **Moon,** would also be noteworthy. Conjunctions involving the Moon, one of the two 'lights', always hold particular importance, as we have previously observed.

What, then, were the planetary configurations at the time of **Cardinal Mazarin's death**? He **passed away on March 9, 1661,** in Paris.

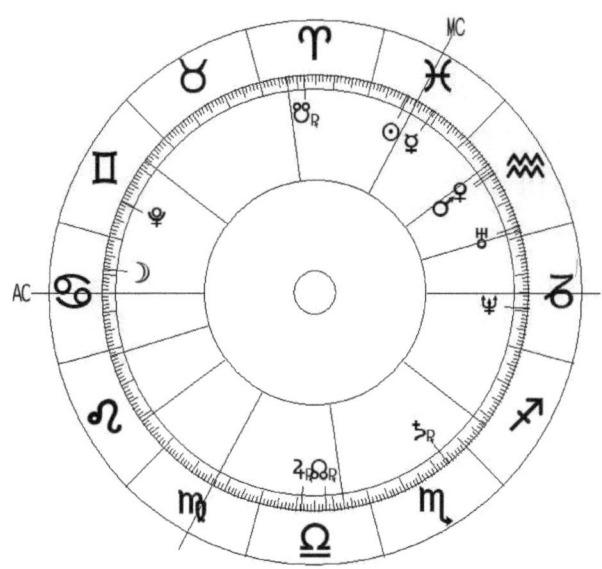

Jules Mazarin – Death on March 9, 1661 (12 noon ?)

At that time, **Mercury** was even closer to the **Sun**. **Neptune**, though still within the same quadrant as the Sun and Mercury, had moved further away, diminishing its significance. However, this was offset by its near-exact **opposition** to the **Moon**, which increased its prominence. From a 'quadrant perspective,' **Neptune** and **Uranus** were in **opposition** to the **Moon** and **Pluto**.

Turning to his next incarnation, Cardinal Mazarin was **reborn on August 31, 1843**, in Darmstadt (Germany) as **Georg Friedrich Count von Hertling**, who served as Chancellor of the German Empire from 1917 to 1918. We aim to investigate whether the Neptunian thread persisted in his horoscope, despite the lack of a precise birth time.

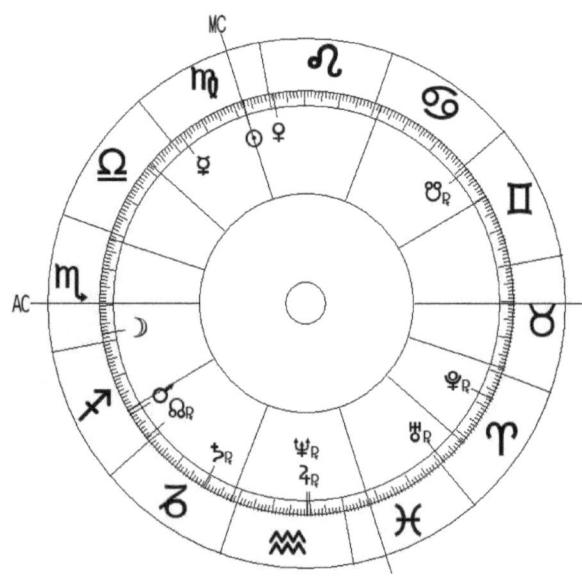

Count von Hertling – Birth on August 31, 1843 (12 noon ?)

Indeed, **Count von Hertling's birth chart** reveals remarkable configurations, with two planetary groups forming in opposing quadrants: **Mercury**, the **Sun**, and **Venus** on one side—ordinarily a common alignment—**opposed** by **Neptune, Jupiter, Uranus**, and **Pluto**. Here, **Neptune** gains increased significance due to its close **conjunction** with the kindred **Jupiter** and especially its **opposition** to the **Sun** and **Venus**.

The Neptunian 'red thread' clearly persisted. The question now arises: Did it extend until Count von Hertling's death? **He died on January 4, 1919**, though no precise time is recorded.

Count von Hertling – Death on January 4, 1919 (12 noon ?)

At first glance, we see an even more pronounced division of planets across two opposing quadrants. **Pluto, Jupiter, Neptune,** and **Saturn** are again clustered in one area of the horoscope. Remarkably, **Neptune** is in an exact degree-aligned (!) **opposition** to the **Moon** and **Mars**, as well as in a broader opposition to the **Sun, Venus,** and **Uranus**.

In both death horoscopes, Uranus and **Mars** maintain similar distances from each other, both times positioned in Aquarius —first in **conjunction with Neptune** (Mazarin) and later in **opposition** (Hertling).

Most striking, however, is the recurrence of the precise **Neptune-Moon opposition** present at **Cardinal Mazarin's death**, reappearing at **Count von Hertling's death** with the same exactitude! This strongly underscores how a 'red thread,' in this case a Neptunian one, can run through multiple lifetimes.

Tommaso Campanella – Otto Weininger

Rudolf Steiner provided an extensive account of three prior incarnations of the Austrian philosopher **Otto Weininger**. Steiner even dedicated an entire lecture within his 1924 karmic studies to the reincarnation path of this individuality. [25]

After Weininger's life as a Jewish woman in the 6th century BCE, during the Babylonian exile of the Jewish people, he was born as a man around the transition from the 5th to the 6th century CE. Steiner elaborates:

---

[25] GA 238 "Esoterische Betrachtungen karmischer Zusammenhänge – Band IV" (Karmic Relationships IV), Dornach, lecture of 21 September 1924

*"But a strange thing arose in that personality who in the pre-Christian centuries had been a woman and was now a man. Because his perceptions and ideas were so vivid, there arose in the man an intense knowledge of how that visionary life which he possessed was connected altogether with the feminine nature. I do not mean to say that the visionary life is in general connected with a woman's personality, but in this case, the whole fundamental character of the visionary life had come over from the former incarnation of the individual as a woman. Thus innumerable secrets were revealed to this man, secrets relating especially to the mutual interaction of **Earth** and **Moon**, secrets relating, for instance, to the life of reproduction. The individuality living in this incarnation as a man became remarkably well versed especially in these domains."*

This unusual personality profile, as described by Steiner, undoubtedly shaped the afterlife of this man. It can be assumed that his experiences in the **Moon sphere** were of particular significance. As we have seen in many instances, such karmic themes are often reflected in the horoscope of a subsequent birth.

The next incarnation of this individuality occurred on **September 5, 1568**, in Stilo, Calabria, as the Italian Dominican friar and philosopher **Tommaso Campanella**. The exact time of birth remains unknown.

Campanella's natal horoscope shows the **Moon** prominently emphasized—not only in **opposition** to the **Sun**, surrounded by a cluster of planets, but also in **conjunction** with the profound **Pluto**. Furthermore, a striking **opposition** exists between **Jupiter** and **Uranus** (on the left in the chart), and **Neptune** (on the right). Whether these planets aligned with the Ascendant or Descendant is uncertain, as the exact birth time is unavailable.

What planetary configurations, then, marked **Campanella's death** 70 years later?

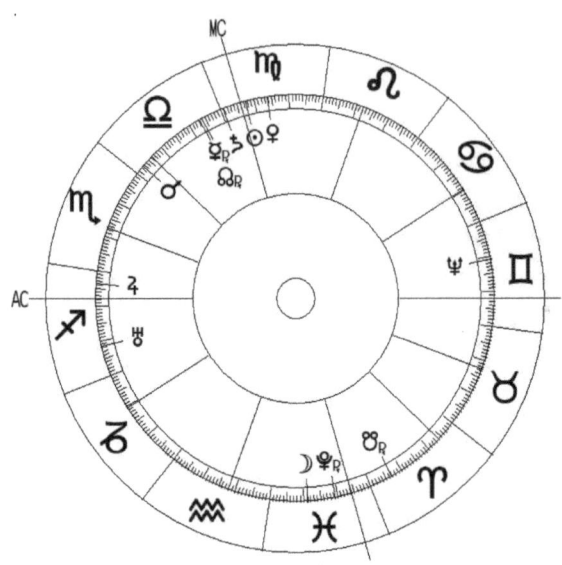

Tommaso Campanella – Birth on September 5, 1568 (12 noon ?)

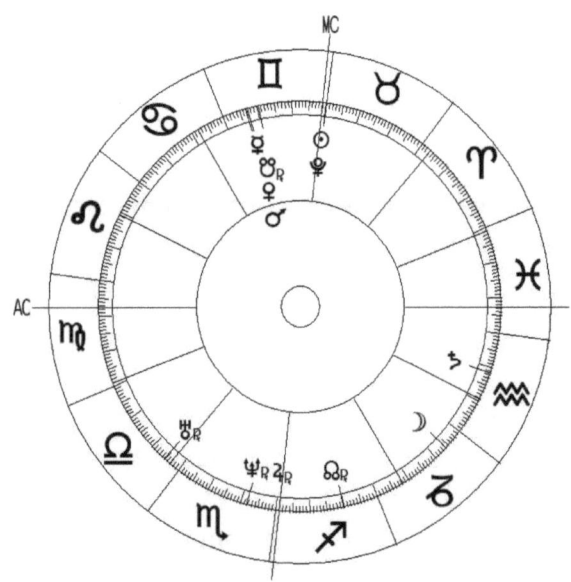

Tommaso Campanella – Death on May 21, 1639 (12 noon ?)

When Campanella **passed away on May 21, 1639**, in Paris, Pluto was in close **conjunction** with the **Sun** and in exact **opposition** to **Jupiter** and **Neptune**, with **Uranus** nearby. This reveals a recurring resonance between his birth and death horoscopes, with **Pluto** playing a pivotal role. **At birth, Pluto** was **conjoined** with the **Moon** and **opposed** the **Sun; at death, Pluto** formed a tight **conjunction** with the **Sun**. Whether Pluto also stood near the Midheaven is unclear, as the lack of an exact time of death necessitated using a default of noon.

Campanella was reborn on **April 3, 1880**, in Vienna as the Austrian philosopher **Otto Weininger**. The birth time given on astro-seek.com is 3:00 PM, which seems plausible since this places **Uranus** at the **Ascendant** and **Pluto** at the **Midheaven** in a square—a fitting astrological signature for Weininger's later tragic suicide. **Mars**, which had aligned with the **descending lunar node** at **Campanella's death**, once again appeared near it at **Weininger's birth**. Additionally, the striking **triple conjunction** of **Saturn, Sun**, and **Mercury** present at **Campanella's birth** reappeared in **Weininger's natal chart**.

On **October 4, 1903**, Otto Weininger took his own life in Beethoven's death room in Vienna, which he had specifically rented for this purpose. His suicide is believed to have occurred during the night or early morning hours. Astrologically, this coincided with a **Uranus transit** at 27° Sagittarius, in **opposition** to **Mars** at 26° Gemini in his **natal chart**. The transiting **Pluto** had also approached his natal **Mars**, reaching 21° Gemini.

The **death horoscope** for Weininger, calculated for 5:00 AM, reveals the ominous alignment: **Uranus** in **opposition** to **Mars**, positioned deep in the sky, while **Pluto** and **Neptune** occupied the Midheaven.

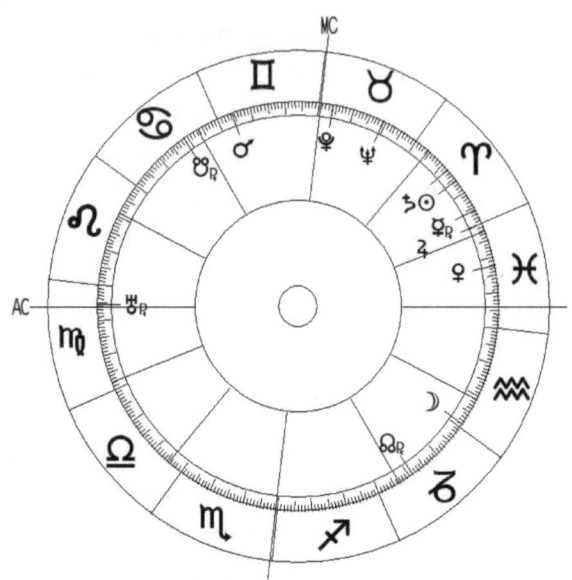

Otto Weininger – Birth on April 3, 1880 at 3:00 p.m. (?)

Otto Weininger – Death on October 4, 1903 (5 a.m. ?)

From the four horoscopes illustrated, it is evident that the karmic 'red thread' in Otto Weininger's incarnations is predominantly marked by **Pluto's** influence.

Ignatius of Loyola – Emanuel Swedenborg

In a lecture delivered on August 24, 1924, in London, Rudolf Steiner unveiled to his audience a prior incarnation of the Swedish scientist and mystic **Emanuel Swedenborg**. He had previously lived as **Ignatius of Loyola**, the founder of the Jesuit Order.

The **birth details** of **Ignatius of Loyola** are sparse; only the year **1491** and the location—Loyola Castle in the Basque Country—are documented. His exact birthdate remains unknown. Steiner described how, in the interval between this previous earthly life and his subsequent birth, Ignatius came *"in touch with a particular Genius, a particular spiritual Being belonging to the* **sphere of Mars**. *[...] Ignatius of Loyola was initially a soldier. He was stricken with a severe illness and in the course of it was inwardly impelled to carry out all kinds of soul-exercises which were the means of filling him with such spiritual strength that he became able to set himself the task of rescuing the old Catholic Christianity from the spread of Evangelicalism."* [26]

For this purpose he founded the 'Society of Jesus', which later became known as the 'Jesuit Order' and *"which immerses Christianity most in earthly-material life."* The distinctive feature of this order lies not only in its exceptionally rigorous spiritual exercises of the will but also in its vow of absolute obedience to the Pope, entailing unconditional submission to his will. The order

---

[26] GA 240 "Esoterische Betrachtungen karmischer Zusammenhänge – Band VI" (Karmic Relationships VI), London, second lecture of 24 August 1924

was organized in a markedly military fashion, entirely founded on the principle of command and obedience.

Astrologically, **Ignatius of Loyola's** character reflected three dominant influences: **Mars** – embodying his military disposition and his initial path as a soldier; **Saturn** – symbolizing his discipline and tenacity, as expressed in his spiritual exercises; **Jupiter** and **Neptune** – representing his deeply religious and mystical-spiritual impulses. We can therefore expect to find these planets highlighted in some way at the end of his life, in his death horoscope.

Ignatius of Loyola **passed away** in Rome on **July 31, 1556**. His **death chart** was created for 12 o'clock due to the lack of a given time:

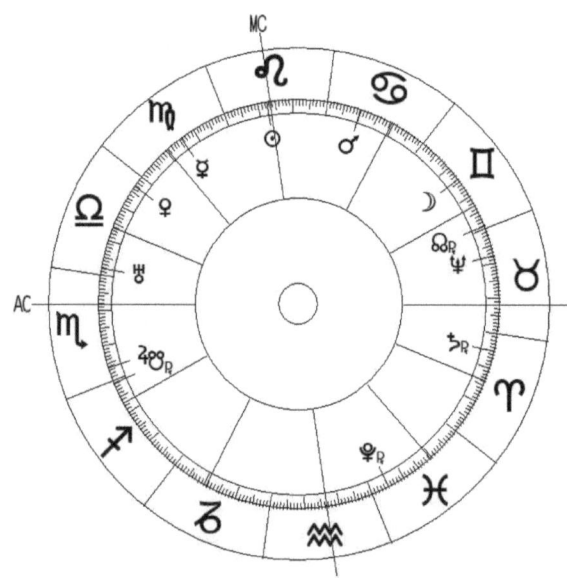

Ignatius von Loyola – Death on July 31, 1556 (12 noon ?)

Rudolf Steiner emphasized the planet **Mars** as particularly significant in relation to **Ignatius of Loyola**, and at the time of Loyola's **death**, **Mars** was near the **Sun**, positioned at the same distance from it as **Mercury**. Both the Mars sphere and the Mercury sphere bear a strong connection to the physical world: the Mars sphere as a region of the spiritual world and the Mercury sphere as a region of the soul world. At Loyola's death, Mercury was at **maximum elongation**, which for the inner planets corresponds to an **opposition**. **Mars** and **Mercury** flanked the **Sun**, with the latter two also in **opposition** to **Pluto**.

Saturn opposed Uranus, possibly emphasized by the proximity to Ascendant and Descendant, but perhaps also to Imum and Medium Coeli, depending on Ignatius's actual birth time.

Neptune stood in **opposition** to **Jupiter**, with their spiritual significance further heightened by their proximity to the **lunar nodes** and **Neptun's conjunction** with the **Moon**.

All connections with the Sun, Moon, or the key points of the horoscope hold particular significance, as we have observed on several occasions. The three most striking characteristics of Ignatius of Loyola listed above are powerfully reflected in his **death horoscope**.

However, his strict spiritual exercises and his intense focus on the earth had a unique posthumous effect. The life review, which normally only lasts a few days after death, remained with him for a much longer period of time. He was, so to speak, in a state of constant retrospection, as Steiner observed:

"After Ignatius Loyola's death, his soul remained always in the vicinity of the earth—for one is near the earth so long as this retrospect lasts. Even if the retrospect is extended it cannot last many centuries for when it extends at all over any long period it is

*quite abnormal—but abnormal things do constantly occur in the great world-connections. And comparatively soon after his earth-life was over, Ignatius Loyola appeared again in the soul of **Emanuel Swedenborg**."*

Remarkably, only 132 years later, Ignatius was reborn on **January 29, 1688** (Julian calendar) in Stockholm. This date corresponds to **February 8, 1688**, under the Gregorian calendar, then gradually replacing the Julian system.

Could planetary configurations so swiftly recreate the three main traits of his prior life? What places did the planets occupy at the **birth** of the scientist and mystic **Emanuel Swedenborg**?

Emanuel Swedenborg
Birth on January 29, 1688 (Julian Calendar)
(12 noon ?)

In **Swedenborg's natal chart** we see **Mars** emphasized, this time due to its proximity to the **Moon**. **Saturn** is again in **opposition** to **Uranus**. Both constellations are enhanced by the integration of the two **lunar nodes**. In addition to this strong opposition, we find a group of planets—**Neptune**, the **Sun**, and **Jupiter—cluster in one quadrant**, **opposing Pluto**.

These aspects echo Ignatius's defining attributes: strength (Mars), perseverance (Saturn), and the religious-spiritual drive (Jupiter-Neptune). The latter only came to the fore in Swedenborg at the age of about 40, when he began to show a completely different side of his nature that seemed very strange to his contemporaries.

*"And so in **Emanuel Swedenborg** we have a man of genius, who gives us brilliant and magnificent description of the lands of the Spirits, albeit in pictures that are somewhat questionable. Thus has the mighty spiritual will of **Ignatius of Loyola** found transformation."*

Swedenborg's death on **March 29, 1772**, in London, further reflects this transformation. His **death chart** reveals:

Mars emphasized, accompanied by the **Moon** and **Jupiter**, but now forming an **opposition** with **Saturn** and **Neptune**. **Jupiter** had drawn even closer to the **Moon** than in his **birth chart**. This is likely to have influenced Swedenborg's afterlife just as much as the close **conjunction** of the **Sun** with **Mercury**, because, as we now know, such conjunctions with the 'lights' always have a special significance.

Venus and **Uranus**, which were together in the same zodiacal sign at the **death of Ignatius of Loyola**, came even closer together at the **death of Emanuel Swedenborg** and united in a close, almost exact **conjunction**, near the descending **lunar node**.

Emanuel Swedenborg – Death on March 29, 1772 (12 noon ?)

Raphael – Novalis

After examining reincarnative connections in a series of historical figures and uncovering some fundamental astrological principles concerning pre-birth existence and subsequent reincarnation, we now venture to consider a truly unique individual: the Italian painter **Raffaello Sanzio**.

Raphael's birth date is disputed. This stems from a statement by *Giorgio Vasari* in 1550, 67 years after Raphael's birth and 30 years after his death. Many of Vasari's claims in his biographies of famous artists[27] have since been scientifically challenged and corrected. Vasari gives Raphael's birth date as *"on **March 28** or **April 6, 1483**, on **Good Friday** at **3 o'clock in the morning**."* In 1483, Good Friday fell on March 28, not April 6. For this reason, Raphael biographers have interpreted Vasari's account as indicating **March 28, 1483, Good Friday**, as Raphael's birth date. Rudolf Steiner concurred with this view:

*"How do people write biographies of Raphael to-day? Even the best are so written that they simply state that Raphael was **born** on **Good Friday** of the year **1483**. It is not for nothing that Raphael was born on a Good Friday. This birth already proclaimed his exceptional position in Christianity and shows that in the deepest and most significant way he was connected with the Christian Mysteries. **It was on a Good Friday that Raphael was born.**"* [28]

Here, Steiner emphasizes the Christian context of Raphael's birth on Good Friday. However, there is a letter from *Marcantonio Michiel* (1484–1552), an art collector born just a year after Raphael, who likely had access to authentic information from Raphael's immediate circle. While the original letter from *Michiel* to *Antonio Marsilio* is lost, it is frequently quoted in art historical works. *Michiel* asserts that Raphael was **born on April 6, 1483**— not on Good Friday—but that he **died** on a **Good Friday** of the same date, **April 6, 1520**. Moreover, he claims Raphael passed away not only on the same day as Christ but also at the same hour: **3 o'clock in the afternoon**, the **hour of Christ's death**, rather than the 3 a.m. cited by *Vasari* for Raphael's birth. However, *Vasari* refers to the time of birth, not death.

---

[27] Giorgio Vasari, "Le Vite de' piu eccellenti pittori, scultori e architettori" (1550, revised 1568)

[28] GA 155 "Christus und die menschliche Seele" (Christ and the Human Soul), Copenhagen, lecture of 23 May 1912

Raphael – Birth on Good Friday, March 28, 1483 (3 a.m. ?)

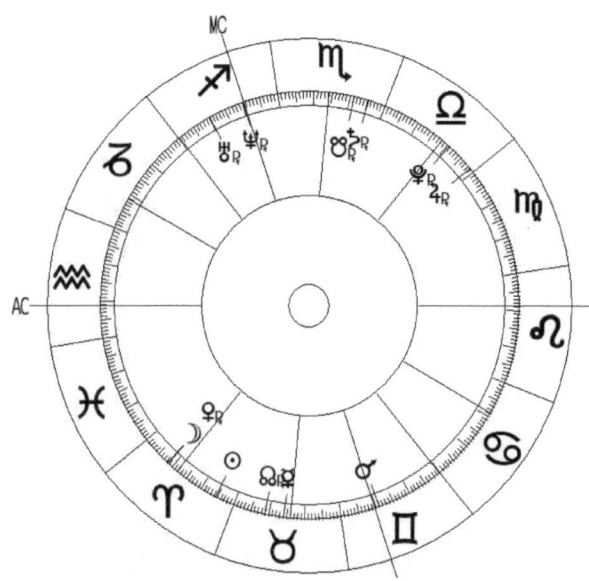

Raphael – Birth on the Sunday after Easter, April 6, 1483 (3 a.m. ?)

We should not disregard Michiel's account, given his proximity to Raphael's era. Thus, we will use it as the basis for a **second, alternative birth horoscope for Raphael** corresponding to **Sunday after Easter, April 6, 1483**. And since we cannot rule out the possibility that Vasari had a reliable source for his claim of "3 a.m." as Raphael's **birth time**, we will tentatively accept this as speculative data.

Rudolf Steiner's emphasis on Raphael's *"exceptional position in Christianity"* and *"that in the deepest and most significant way he was connected with the Christian Mysteries"* would apply to his **death** on Good Friday, and at the hour of Christ's death, just as much as to his **birth** on a Good Friday.

According to Rudolf Steiner, Raphael was a reincarnation of **John the Baptist**, a relative of Jesus of Nazareth. This enabled Raphael to depict numerous deeply moving images of Mary and the Christ Child with inner spiritual vision. In his painting *Madonna Terranuova*, Raphael even portrays Mary with two Jesus boys. [29]

If Vasari's specified birth time of "3 a.m." is accurate, **Uranus** and **Neptune** would have been in a prominent position at the **Medium Coeli** in both of Raphael's possible **birth horoscopes**. If born on **Good Friday, March 28, 1483**, these planets would be further elevated by their **conjunction** with the **Moon**. This enhancement would remain significant regardless of the exact hour of birth. Such conjunctions and oppositions involving the 'lights' have proven critical in previous analyses. Thus, the astrological considerations of Raphael's potential birth dates

---

[29] "Madonna Terranuova", painted by Raphael when he was only 21/22 years old, around 1505. The painting is part of the permanent exhibition in the Gemäldegalerie (Painting Gallery) Berlin. – On the subject of the "two Jesus boys", see, for example, Rudolf Steiner's lectures on the Gospel of Luke (GA 114) and the Gospel of Matthew (GA 123).

support Steiner's claim of a Good Friday birth in 1483. Remarkably, Raphael would then have been born and died on a Good Friday.

In astrology, **Neptune** represents supersensory perception. The **Uranus sphere** is the first region beyond the traditional seven planets. It corresponds to the fourth region of the spiritual world which is associated with the *I*, the fourth human principle.

As detailed in the author's book *Ancient and Modern Worldview – Rudolf Steiner's Criticism of Astrology* [30], the **Uranus sphere** is the source of the zodiacal forces of our solar system. Every solar system has its own zodiac. In our case, the Saturn sphere emerged as the first during the formation of our planetary system. Just as the Sun mediates between the inner and outer planets, the zodiac associated with the region of the Uranus orbit mediates between the intra-systemic planetary forces and the extra-systemic stellar forces. The latter are an expression of the Cosmic Word or Christ. We know this from the New Testament account of the parables of the Feeding of the Four Thousand and the Five Thousand, representing the peoples of the fourth and fifth post-Atlantean cultural epochs. The two fish symbolize the forces of the zodiac sign Pisces, while the loaves, as 'heavenly bread,' represent the forces of the remaining zodiac signs of our zodiac. [31]

The forces of the *I* act from this region as the primary shapers of the human form. They organize it according to the principles of twelve and seven, corresponding to the 12 zodiacal signs and the 7 planetary spheres. This is reflected in Uranus's orbital period, as it takes 12 x 7 = 84 years to complete one full orbit. Following this law, human life on earth also proceeds in periods of seven years.

---

[30] Publisher BoD (Books on Demand GmbH), Norderstedt

[31] See, for example, GA 123 "Das Matthäus-Evangelium" (The Gospel of St. Matthew), Bern, lecture of 10 September 1910

We can see from this the immense formative power inherent in the zodiac.

The 'I forces' find their clearest expression in the human face. And since they are connected to the planet **Uranus**, these forces reveal themselves most clearly in the sign it rules: **Aquarius**. The clairvoyant humanity of ancient times therefore perceived a human face when looking in the direction of Aquarius, similar to what has been preserved in many churches as one of the evangelists' symbols.

The great herald of Christ, the Cosmic Word, and his *I*-creating power, was **John the Baptist**. Assuming, based on Rudolf Steiner's repeated statements, that the individuality of **John the Baptist** reincarnated in **Raphael**, it is not surprising that **Uranus** holds a prominent position not only in his **birth chart** but also in his **death chart**. In the latter, we find **Uranus** in **conjunction** with the **Sun** instead of the Moon, and additionally in **conjunction** with the **ascending lunar node**. Evidently, the karmic 'red thread' in the individuality of **John the Baptist – Raphael** is strongly influenced by **Uranus**.

In this case, one should assume that Uranus would also be found in a prominent position in the horoscopes of the subsequent incarnation of Raphael, the German poet Novalis. What Raphael expressed in moving paintings, Novalis conveyed centuries later in equally moving poems, such as his *Spiritual Songs* or *Hymns to the Night*, describing supersensory experiences.

Novalis, born as **Georg Philipp Friedrich von Hardenberg** on **May 2, 1772**, at Oberwiederstedt Castle (Germany), has no recorded birth time. His **natal horoscope** is calculated for noon.

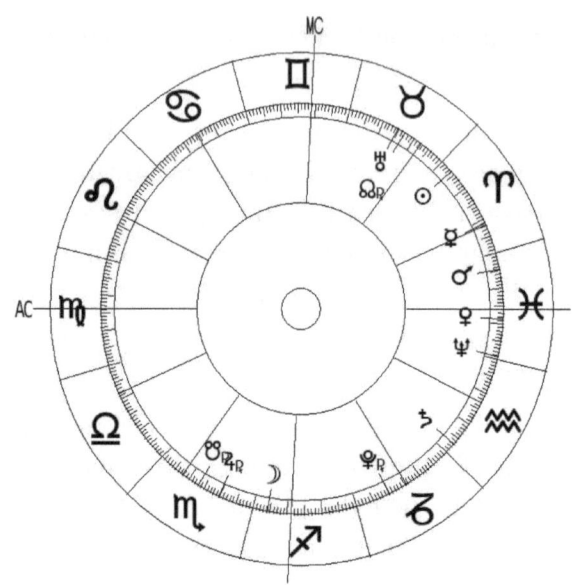

Raphael – Death on April 6, 1520, Good Friday at 3 p.m.

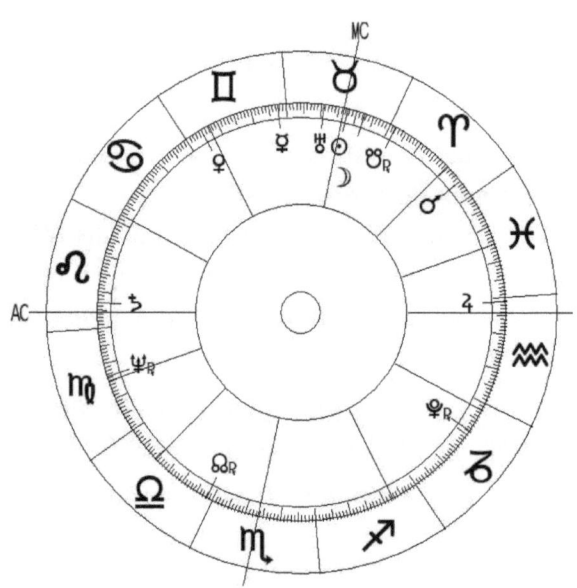

Novalis – Birth on May 22, 1772 (12 noon ?)

The most striking feature of **Novalis' birth chart** is the **conjunction** of **Uranus** with both (!) 'lights', the **Sun** and **Moon**, again near a **lunar node**. If he were born around midday, this planetary grouping would also align with the Medium Coeli.

Uranus' placement at **Novalis' birth** is particularly significant. In 1772, Uranus was at 19° Taurus, only 4° from its position at **Raphael's death** (15° Taurus). At least, this is what is stated in the ephemerides.

However, at the time of **Raphael's death**, the vernal point had already retrograded by 1.5° into the area of Pisces. The Sun no longer rose at 0° Aries at the spring equinox, as the ephemerides rigidly and immovably suggest, completely disregarding (!) the precession of the equinox, for all centuries. Instead, it rose at 28.5° Pisces. This retrograde shift affects all planetary positions, as the distances between the planets remain unaffected by it.

Therefore, for **Raphael's year of death in 1520**, we must subtract 1.5° from 15° Taurus, which gives us the true position of **Uranus** at **13.5° Taurus**. By the time of **Novalis' birth in 1772**, the vernal point had already retrograded by 5° into Pisces. Thus, we must subtract these 5° from 19° Taurus, the position for Uranus as given in the ephemerides, resulting in **14° Taurus**. [32] Consequently, **Uranus was once again at the same position at Novalis' birth as it had been at Raphael's death!** In the meantime, Uranus had completed three full cycles through the zodiac. This provides a truly impressive confirmation of the

---

[32] See the table of correction values in the author's books "Influences of the Forces of the Zodiac on the Cultural Development of Mankind" (Fig. 6, p. 39) and "Ancient and Modern World View – Rudolf Steiner's Criticism of Astrology" (Fig. 4, p. 53), Publisher BoD (Books on Demand), Norderstedt, Germany

Uranus-influenced karmic 'red thread' in the individuality of Raphael-Novalis.

The planets **Jupiter** and **Pluto** were in close **conjunction** at **Raphael's birth** and, at the time of his **death**, they were still within a common quadrant, similar to their alignment at **Novalis' birth**.

What about the situation 29 years later, at **Novalis' death** on **March 25, 1801**, in Weißenfels? His death reportedly occurred "in the late evening." Therefore, we speculatively use 11:00 PM to create the **death chart**. Indeed, it is striking that **Uranus** is once again emphasized, this time in **opposition** to the **Sun** and again in conjunction with a lunar node. The 'karmic thread' continues to act. If Novalis died around 11:45 PM, Uranus would even have been exactly at the Medium Coeli.

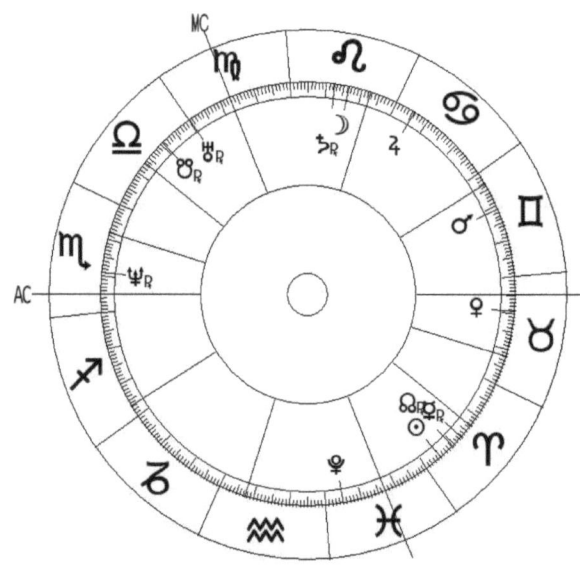

Novalis – Death on March 25, 1801 (11 p.m. ?)

Francisco de Almeida – Walter Johannes Stein

We now turn to individuals of the 20th century who played significant roles within the Anthroposophical Society.

Walter Johannes Stein provided significant support to Rudolf Steiner in his efforts to promote the "Threefold Social Organism," which envisioned the separation of the cultural, legal, and economic spheres into independent domains. In the 1930s, several years after Rudolf Steiner's death, Stein left Germany and moved to England. There, he worked in the economic domain alongside *Daniel Nicol Dunlop* in the *World Power Conference*, founded by Dunlop (now the *World Energy Council*), aiming for the peaceful utilization and development of global energy resources. Stein's active international engagement mirrors what seems like a continuation of his prior incarnation as the Portuguese navigator, governor, and viceroy of Portuguese India, **Francisco de Almeida**, who played a key role in overseas trade between Europe and the colonies in India and Southeast Asia.

In 1924, during a trip to Portugal, **Walter Johannes Stein** experienced what he described as a retrospective vision of his previous life. Rudolf Steiner affirmed the validity of this experience. Stein wrote about it in one of his many autobiographical notes:

"Insight into previous earthly lives is granted through grace. When I spoke with Dr. Steiner about such an experience, he said, «You have relived your last death.»" [33]

It is important to pay close attention to Rudolf Steiner's precise wording. Stein's experience is commonly interpreted as a direct

---

[33] Johannes Tautz, "W. J. Stein – eine Biographie", p. 263

view of his former life. However, such direct retrospection is accessible only to a select few on an advanced spiritual path. More frequently, individuals on lower stages of spiritual initiation may recall events from the interlude between incarnations. After all, our pre-birth sphere experiences are reflected in the septennial phases of our earthly lives, as the author illustrates in a book based on his own biography. [34]

A particularly profound experience in the higher spheres is the enduring retrospection of the previous death. While we cannot remember our birth during earthly life, in the interval between incarnations, the memory of our last death remains a vivid image before us. According to Rudolf Steiner, witnessing the triumph of spirit over matter or life over death is one of the most uplifting impressions of our existence in the spheres. It is highly probable that W. J. Stein's experience on June 27, 1924, was precisely this. He wrote:

*"One might think it a terrifying experience to relive one's own death (I mean the last death prior to this life). But it is not so. It is a blissful experience. I relived the murder of an old man. He was the captain of a ship and met his end ascending the steps from the ship's interior to its deck. There, amid ropes and masts, he was struck by his enemy's spear—a peculiarly shaped ceremonial spear with a wavy blade. It pierced him above the teeth of his upper jaw and killed him instantly. I experienced this in every detail: the landscape—it was just **sunset**—, the uniform of the old man with its ornate metal buttons, his heavy steps as he climbed the stairs.*

What struck me most was the marvelous ease with which the soul left the body, rather than the man who cast the spear. Yet my

---

[34] Roland Schrapp, "The Mirroring of Life before Birth in the Seven-Year Periods of Human Life on Earth", Publisher BoD (Books on Demand), Norderstedt

love and gratitude poured out to him. One might not expect to feel gratitude toward one's killer. And yet it is so." [35]

This account aligns in detail with how **Francisco de Almeida** died on **March 1, 1510**, during his return voyage from India to Portugal. He was **killed** by a spear while standing on the deck of his ship in South Africa's Saldanha Bay at sunset. Although the exact time of his death is not historically recorded, Stein's description suggests it occurred around **6:20 PM**, the local sunset time. While only Almeida's birth year and location (1450 in Lisbon) are known, his death is well-documented, allowing for a credible **death horoscope** to be constructed.

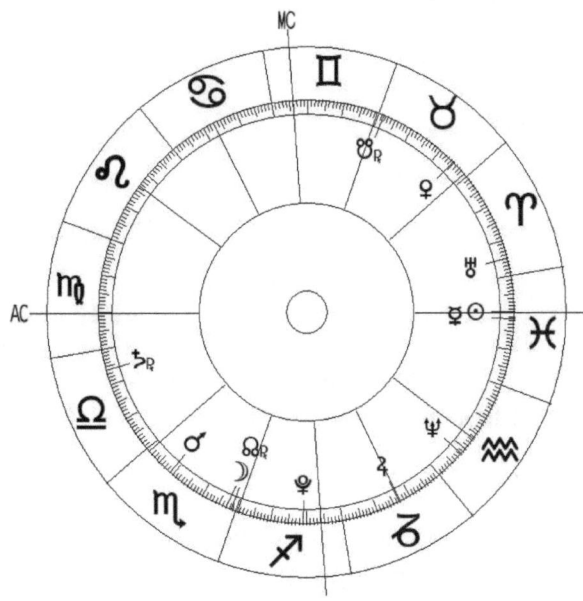

Francisco de Almeida
Death on March 1, 1510 around 6:20 p.m.

---

[35] Johannes Tautz, "W. J. Stein – eine Biographie", p. 263

On **February 6, 1891**, the individuality of Francisco de Almeida was reborn in Vienna under the name **Walter Johannes Stein**. The time of birth is unknown. His birth horoscope was therefore drawn up for 12 noon.

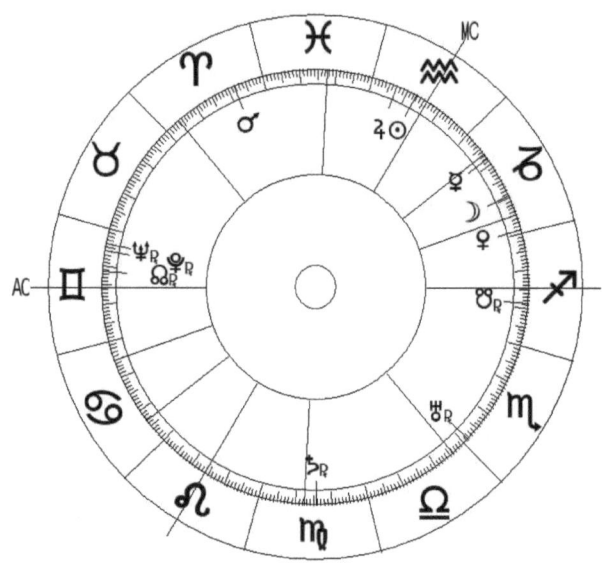

Walter Johannes Stein
Birth on February 6, 1891 (12 noon ?)

At first glance, there appears to be little correlation between **Almeida's death horoscope** and **Stein's birth horoscope**. The positions of the Sun and Moon are significantly different. Planetary emphasis by proximity to the horoscope's angular points is assessable only in **Almeida's death chart**, as the time of **sunset** provides a precise reference. On March 1, 1510, the **Sun** and **Mercury** set together, followed by **Uranus**, while **Saturn** approached its rise in the east. This highlights these planets.

According our insights from previous horoscope comparisons, we can observe, in **Almeida's death horoscope**, that **Uranus**—emphasized by its proximity to the **Sun**, **Mercury**, and the **Descendant**—was in wide **conjunction** with **Venus** and in **opposition** to **Saturn** and **Mars**. The **Uranus-Saturn opposition** was nearly exact, suggesting that **Uranus** serves as the karmic 'red thread' in this case, with its aspects to **Saturn**, **Mars**, and **Venus** also playing a significant role.

In **Stein's natal horoscope**, **Mars** is in **opposition** to **Uranus** and **Saturn**. **Mars** occupies 8° Aries, with its opposing point, 8° Libra, falling between **Uranus** and **Saturn**. This demonstrates again that traditional astrological rules for aspect orbs, which demand narrow degrees, do not apply in such cases. They are probably generally beyond reality when it comes to interpreting horoscopes. It may also explain why Rudolf Steiner regarded much of contemporary astrology as *"that almost everything that is nowadays practiced in this area is the purest dilettantism—a true superstition—and that, as far as the world at large is concerned, the true science of these things has largely been lost!"* [36]

If connections between a **death horoscope** and a subsequent **birth horoscope** are not immediately apparent, as in this case, it is always worthwhile to examine **the next death horoscope** in the sequence.

---

[36] GA 15 "Die geistige Führung des Menschen und der Menschheit" (The Spiritual Guidance of Mankind), Copenhagen, third lecture (8 June 1911). The stenographic transcripts of these lectures were personally revised by Rudolf Steiner for publication. – See also Roland Schrapp "Ancient and Modern World View – Rudolf Steiner's Criticism of Astrology", Publisher BoD (Books on Demand), Norderstedt

Walter Johannes Stein passed away on **July 7, 1957**, at **1:20** or **1:25 AM** in London, as reported by a night nurse. [37] His **death horoscope** reveals a striking resemblance to Almeida's: the **Sun-Mercury conjunction** appears once again, with **Uranus** in close proximity. Moreover, **Uranus** forms a conspicuous **conjunction** with **Mars** and **Venus**. Recall that in **Almeida's death horoscope**, **Venus** and **Uranus** opposed **Mars** and **Saturn**, with **Venus** and **Mars** in direct **opposition**.

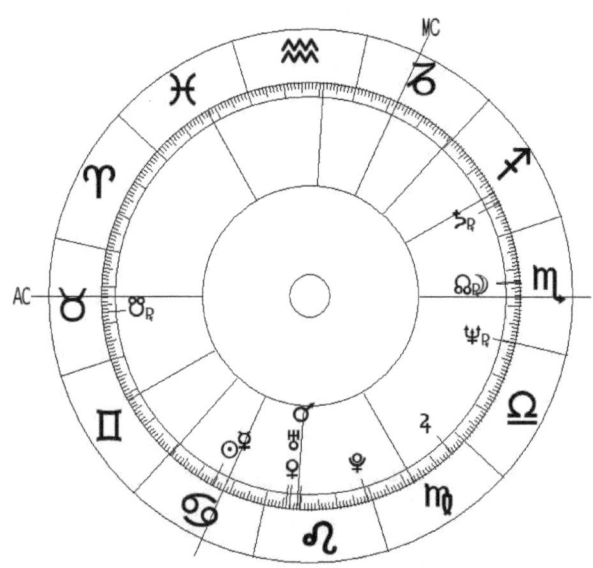

Walter Johannes Stein – Death on July 7, 1957 at 1:20 a.m.

Taken together, the three horoscopes show a much stronger resemblance than initially apparent. Proper interpretation of planetary aspects, without reliance on outdated astrological conventions, is crucial.

---

[37] Johannes Tautz, "W. J. Stein – eine Biographie", p. 256

Finally, it is worth noting another significant detail. Stein's aforementioned 'retrospective' experience occurred in 1924, when he was 33 years old, in the sixth year of his fifth septennium. However, it is known that he had already been contemplating an earlier incarnation in the 9th century, which led him to an in-depth study of that period. This ultimately culminated in his book *The Ninth Century and the Holy Grail*. Stein's soul was deeply engaged with questions about his previous earthly lives.

Answers to such inquiries are most accessible during the eighth septennium of life when our pre-birth experiences in the sphere of the Spirit Self are mirrored. In this sphere, we have a comprehensive overview of our incarnational sequence. The Spirit Self corresponds to our fifth member of being, and each year of a septennium correlates to one of our components. Thus, the fifth year of every septennium is especially connected to the Spirit Self, making it an optimal time to receive insights—both coming to us from outside and inside—about our past incarnations. The author has explored this phenomenon in detail in his book *The Mirroring of Life before Birth in the Seven-Year Periods of Human Life on Earth*, using examples from his own life journey.

If W. J. Stein experienced his aforementioned 'retrospective' in the sixth year of his fifth septennium, at the age of 33, it was surely prepared in the depths of his soul during the preceding fifth year. It only manifested with a delay in the following year. And it was exactly *one* septennium later when he undertook his long-planned journey to Portugal to delve into his prior incarnation as Francisco de Almeida.

Emperor Frederick II – Guenther Wachsmuth

Another close collaborator of Rudolf Steiner was **Guenther Wachsmuth**, who, upon Steiner's suggestion, was elected to the first executive council of the newly founded General Anthroposophical Society during the Christmas Conference of 1923, despite being only 30 years old at the time. Prior to this, Wachsmuth had served as Steiner's secretary and constant traveling companion. After Steiner's death, Wachsmuth was one of the four pallbearers.[38] In the years that followed, he devoted significant energy to completing the second Goetheanum.

Like many anthroposophists in Steiner's inner circle, Guenther Wachsmuth spent years researching his prior incarnation. According to Wachsmuth, Rudolf Steiner once responded to his inquiry on the matter with the statement: *"Southern Italy, 13th century— a knight."*[39] Ultimately, Wachsmuth came to the conclusion that he had lived as **Frederick II of Hohenstaufen**, King of Sicily and Southern Italy and later Holy Roman Emperor, during the 13th century. This realization sparked a deep desire in Wachsmuth to visit Southern Italy, Frederick II's homeland. While on a health retreat in Ascona, Switzerland, in 1961, he meticulously planned a trip for the following year. Wachsmuth was then 67 years old, entering the fifth year of his ninth seven-year period.

The connection between such a fifth year, and the Spirit Self— the fifth constituent element of the human being—and the sphere of the Spirit Self, where we gain an overview of our incarnations,

---

[38] The other three bearers of Rudolf Steiner's coffin were Ehrenfried Pfeiffer, Georg Groot and Edmund Pracht.

[39] Heinz Herbert Schöffler, "Guenther Wachsmuth – Ein Lebensbild" (Guenther Wachsmuth – A Portrait of His Life), p. 205, Verlag am Goetheanum

was already discussed at the end of the previous chapter. Ultimately, Guenther Wachsmuth was unable to carry out his meticulously planned journey due to his progressively worsening illness.

A man of many talents, Wachsmuth not only possessed exceptional organizational skills but also wrote dramas. His final play, *Archangels in Council*, revolves around the celestial council of Platonists and Aristotelians at the turn of the 12th to the 13th century, a theme described by Rudolf Steiner in his karma lectures. The drama includes scenes from the life of Frederick II, who lived on Earth during that time, with the epilogue depicting him on his deathbed, reflecting on his own existence. This demonstrates how deeply convinced Guenther Wachsmuth was of his previous incarnation.

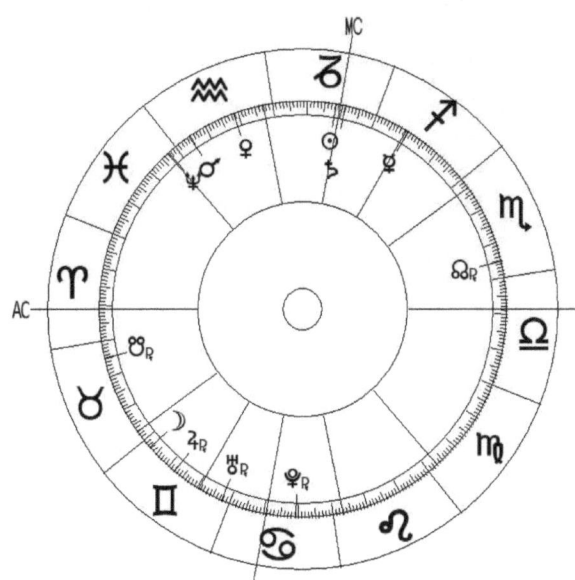

Frederick II – Birth on December 26, 1194 (12 noon ?)

Frederick II was **born** on **December 26, 1194**, in Jesi, Southern Italy (near Ancona). In the absence of a recorded birth time, his above **natal chart** was constructed for noon. We focus again primarily on conjunctions and oppositions as well as the **Sun** and **Moon**. The close conjunction of the **Sun** with **Saturn** immediately catches our eye, indicative of an extended prenatal sojourn in the Saturn sphere. The **Sun-Saturn** alignment is further emphasized by an opposition to **Uranus** and **Pluto**, which were near each other. Additionally, noteworthy are the **Mars-Neptune** and **Moon-Jupiter conjunctions**, with **Jupiter** positioned between the Moon and Uranus.

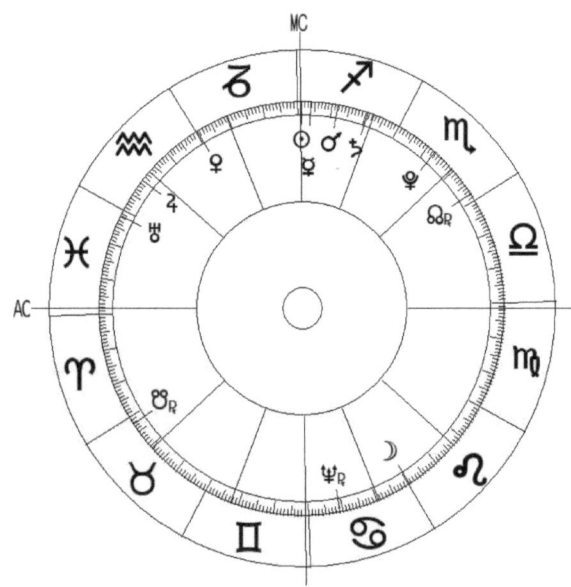

Frederick II – Death on December 13, 1250 (12 noon ?)

At **Frederick II's death** on **December 13, 1250**, at Castel Fiorentino near Lucera (Southern Italy, then part of the Kingdom of Sicily), **Saturn** was again near the **Sun**, echoing the Sun-Saturn conjunction of his natal chart. **Pluto**, previously in opposition to the Sun, had drawn nearer, and the **Mars-Neptune conjunction** had shifted to an **opposition**.

The **Moon-Jupiter conjunction** at **Frederick's birth** transformed into a **Moon-Neptune conjunction** at his **death**. Such an exchange between Jupiter and Neptune can often be observed. This is likely possible due to their inherent affinity, as both govern the same zodiac signs. However, **Jupiter** remained linked to the **Moon-Neptune conjunction** through an **opposing position**. In this way, Jupiter was able to reestablish its **birth conjunction** with **Uranus** at the time of **Frederick's death**. **Mars** and **Mercury** have moved closer to the Sun and joined the **Sun-Saturn conjunction**.

When **Guenther Wachsmuth** was **born** on **October 4, 1893**, the striking **Sun-Saturn-Mars-Mercury conjunction**, already noted at the **death of Frederick II**, reappeared.

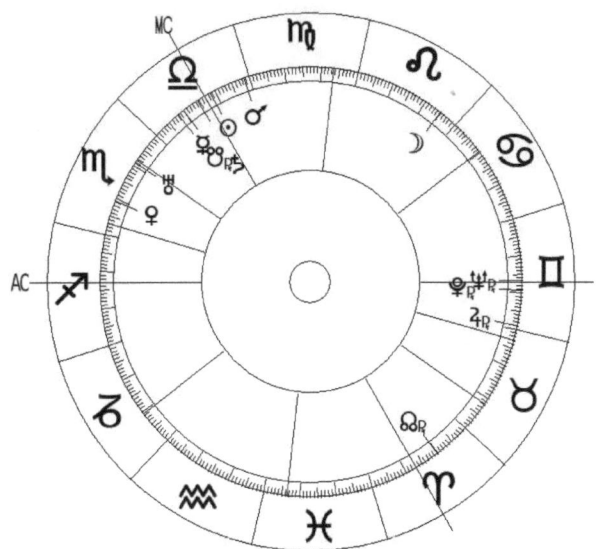

Guenther Wachsmuth – Birth on October 4, 1893 (12 noon ?)

Additionally, a **lunar node** joined this major conjunction. The **Sun** and **Saturn** were not only closely aligned at **Frederick II's death** but had already been in a **very tight conjunction** at his **birth**. This suggests that **Saturn** serves as the karmic 'red thread' here.

Another fascinating detail is **Uranus's** proximity to the **Sun-Saturn-Mars-Mercury conjunction** at **Wachsmuth's birth**. Apparently, Uranus is also trying to connect with the **Sun**.

At **Wachsmuth's death on March 2, 1963**, around **9 p.m.**, **Uranus** and **Pluto opposed** the **Sun** and **Jupiter**, with **Saturn** remaining near the **Sun**. This planetary arrangement bears a striking resemblance to **Frederick II's natal chart**, where **Uranus** and **Pluto**, along with **Jupiter**, opposed the **Sun** and **Saturn**.

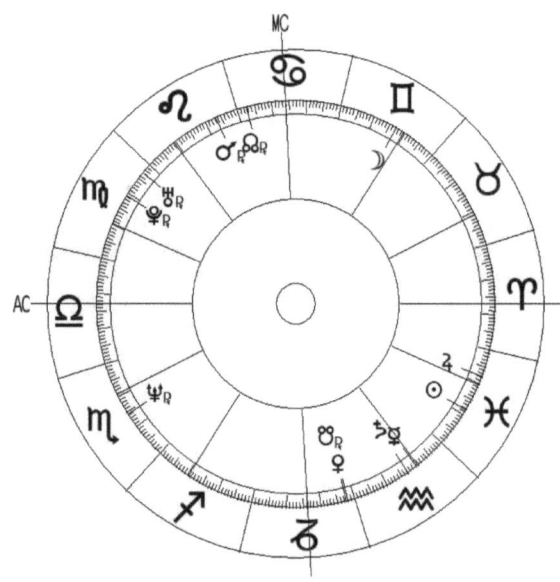

Guenther Wachsmuth – Death on March 2, 1963 around 9 p.m.

Obviously, there are not only relationships between a death horoscope and the immediately following birth horoscope, but also strikingly similar planetary positions, almost a repetition of the configurations from the birth chart of the previous incarnation in the death chart of the subsequent incarnation! This reveals the profound kinship between these horoscopes.

This interconnectedness becomes even more evident through another planetary grouping. **Frederick II's birth chart** features a **Venus-Sun-Saturn-Mercury** grouping, which reappears in **Wachsmuth's death chart** with minor alterations as **Venus-Saturn-Mercury-Sun**.

Neptune, near this group in **Frederick II's natal chart**, was replaced by the related **Jupiter** in **Wachsmuth's death chart**, aligning with the **Sun**.

Similarly, **Mars**, located in the same quadrant as this grouping in **Frederick II's birth chart**, maintained its connection in **Wachsmuth's death chart** by **opposing** the group.

These recurring alignments—whether through conjunctions or oppositions—illustrate the underlying relationships between the charts.

Furthermore, it can be observed that **Jupiter** sometimes takes **Neptune's** place due to their inherent affinity, as both rule Pisces and Sagittarius.

Mars and **Pluto** are also related in nature. They rule together in the zodiacal signs of Aries and Scorpio. Accordingly, **Pluto** sometimes takes the place of **Mars** when a new incarnation is to occur. At the **birth of Frederick II**, for example, there was a **Mars-Neptune conjunction**. At his **death** it was changed to the **opposition Mars-Neptune** and finally varied to the **conjunction Pluto-Neptune** at the **birth of Guenther Wachsmuth**.

These transformations are essential, as the great mobility of the planets makes it challenging to align the necessary configurations for a subsequent incarnation.

Giotto di Bondone – Albert Steffen

The exact birth date of the Italian painter **Giotto di Bondone** remains uncertain; even the year is a matter of debate, likely falling between 1265 and 1276 in Vespignano (Vicchio). As a young boy, he became a pupil of the esteemed painter *Cimabue*. **Giotto passed away on January 8, 1337**, in Florence, allowing for the calculation of his **death horoscope**.

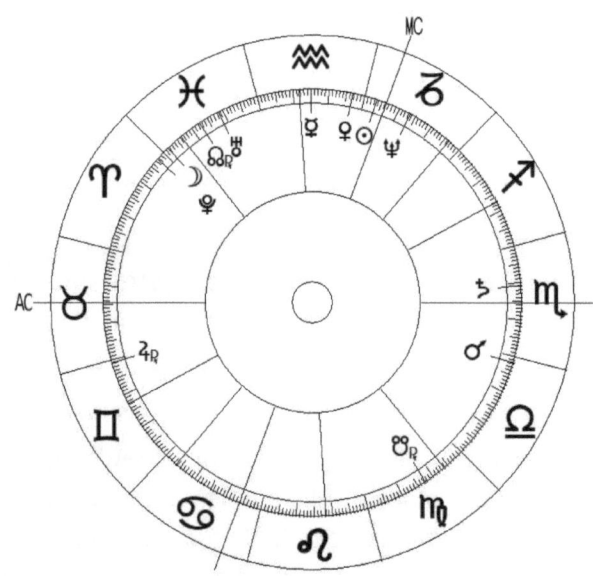

Giotto – Death on January 8, 1337 (12 noon ?)

The prominent configurations involving the 'lights' include **Neptune's conjunction** with the **Sun** and **Venus**, as well as the **Uranus-Pluto conjunction** with the **Moon** and the **ascending lunar node. Jupiter** was in **opposition** to **Mars** and **Saturn**.

We are informed about **Giotto's** next incarnation thanks to a clear statement made by Rudolf Steiner in a letter he wrote from the Goetheanum to his wife, Marie Steiner, who was then in Berlin, on February 27, 1927:

*"To understand **Steffen**, one must reflect on him as **Giotto**. The transition from Cimabue to G. represents a shift from luminous spiritualism—spirituality expressed through colour, perception, and form—to naturalism. Only in Raphael and a few great artists does something of what was lost remain, preserved faintly in Cimabue. This is mirrored in Steffen's psyche. He works with forces that well up in him as a result of the transition at that time, engaging with reality in a way that is actually only possible in the twentieth century. G. had the beauty before him, from which he grew. This idealized his naturalism. Steffen has been surrounded by artlessness, which materializes the spiritualism dormant within him from the beginning. And the fact that Steffen is present among us: I also see a significant karma in that."* [40]

At the suggestion of Rudolf Steiner, the poet and writer **Albert Steffen** was elected to the first board of the newly founded General Anthroposophical Society at the Christmas Conference in 1923, as deputy chairman of the society and head of the Section for the Fine Arts at the Goetheanum.

Albert Steffen was born on December 10, 1884, in Ober-murgenthal near Wynau, Canton Bern, Switzerland. In his **birth**

---

[40] GA 262 "Rudolf Steiner – Marie Steiner-von Sivers / Briefwechsel und Dokumente 1901 – 1925" (Correspondence with Marie Steiner 1901-1925), p. 450 f.

chart, we see **Uranus** again in **conjunction** with the **Moon**, this time almost exactly, and also, as at **Giotto's death**, together with the **ascending lunar node**. These three have come together again.

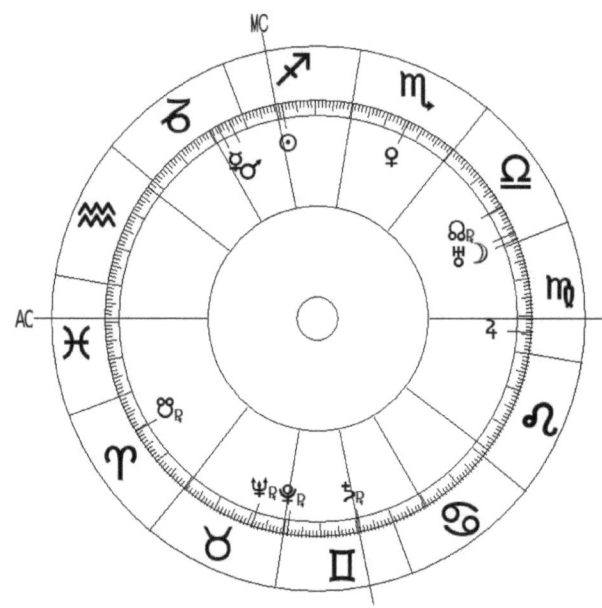

Albert Steffen – Birth on December 10, 1884 (12 noon ?)

Pluto now joins **Neptune**, whose earlier conjunction with the **Sun** is mirrored in **opposition**. **Pluto** replaces its previous connection with the night light **'Moon'** by aligning with the day light **'Sun'**, maintaining its prominence through these celestial lights. **Mars** and **Saturn**, **conjoined at Giotto's death**, appear in **opposition** in **Steffen's birth chart**.

As so often, we observe conjunctions and oppositions of the planets alternating in consecutive incarnations.

At **Giotto's death, Jupiter** was about 60° from the **Moon**. By **Steffen's birth,** this distance had halved to less than 30°.

When **Albert Steffen passed away on July 13, 1963**, at the age of 79 in Dornach, **Jupiter** and the **Moon** had formed a complete **conjunction**.

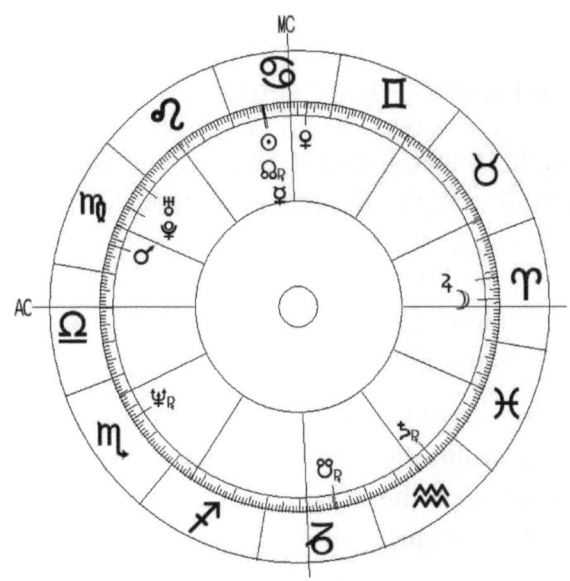

Albert Steffen – Death on July 13, 1963 (12 noon ?)

The **Uranus-Pluto conjunction** from **Giotto's death** reoccurred, this time accompanied by **Mars**, forming an **opposition** to **Saturn**.

The karmic 'red thread' of the individuality of Giotto-Steffen seems to be **Uranus-** and/or **Pluto**-focused. This gave both death horoscopes their distinct shape. In **Albert Steffen's birth chart**, the two planets are indeed separate from each other, but they are still strengthened through their connection to the **Sun** and the **Moon**, respectively.

The astrological analysis of these three charts strongly supports Rudolf Steiner's assertion regarding Albert Steffen's earlier incarnation as Giotto di Bondone.

Reginald of Piperno – Ita Wegman

One of Rudolf Steiner's closest companions was the physician **Ita Wegman**. During the Christmas Conference of 1923, she was appointed as one of the board members of the new society and entrusted with leading the Medical Section at the Goetheanum. Furthermore, Rudolf Steiner chose her as co-leader of the First Class of the School of Spiritual Science.

Ita Wegman was one of Rudolf Steiner's closest esoteric pupils. As we know from documents in her estate, he repeatedly encouraged her over the years to research her karmic past and their shared previous incarnations.

Margarete Kirchner-Bockholt, also a physician and a former close collaborator of Ita Wegman, along with her husband *Erich*, reported in a privately printed work for members of the General Anthroposophical Society about a series of shared earthly lives of Rudolf Steiner with Ita Wegman. [41] She is said to have lived in her immediate prior incarnation in the 13th century as the Dominican **Reginald of Piperno** in Italy. Starting' in 1260, he served for fourteen years as the personal secretary, constant companion, and

---

[41] Margarete und Erich Kirchner-Bockholt "Die Menschheitsaufgabe Rudolf Steiners und Ita Wegman Ita" (Rudolf Steiner's Mission and Ita Wegman), Philosophisch-Anthroposophischer Verlag am Goetheanum, Dornach 1981

cell neighbor of *Thomas Aquinas* (later Rudolf Steiner). Reginald was also the one who heard Thomas's confession on his deathbed and arranged his burial.

A comparison of the planetary positions in the horoscopes of **Reginald of Piperno** and his subsequent incarnation as **Ita Wegman** would be highly interesting. Unfortunately, no reliable birth or death dates for Reginald from the 13th century have been passed down to us. He is said to have been born around 1230 in Piperno (now Priverno), Italy, and to have died around 1290 in Anagni. Thus, we are left with the possibility of examining the **birth and death horoscopes** of Ita Wegman for similarities.

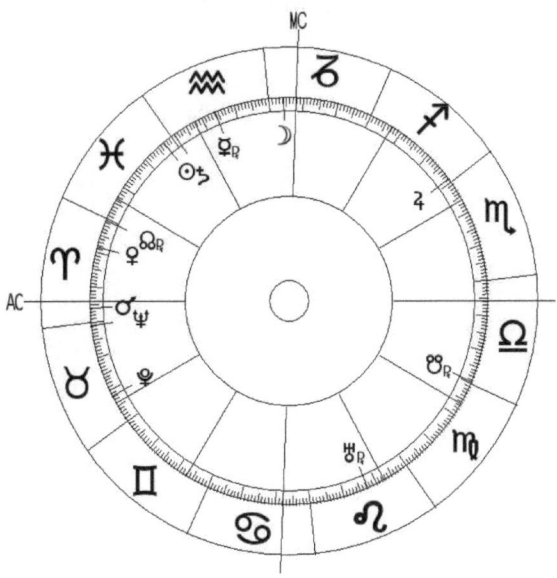

Ita Wegman – Birth on February 22, 1876 around 9:30 a.m.

Ita Wegman was born on February 22, 1876, in Karawang on the island of Java (then Dutch East Indies, now Indonesia). According to her brother-in-law Hupkes, her time of birth was

9:30 or 9:40 AM.[42] **She died on March 4, 1943**, in Arlesheim (Switzerland). The exact time of her death is not known to the author. Therefore, her death horoscope was calculated for midday.

In her **birth horoscope**, an **opposition** between **Saturn** and **Uranus** stands out, emphasized by the **conjunction** of **Saturn** with the **Sun**. The connection between **Saturn** and **Uranus** is also present in her **death horoscope**. While both have moved away from the **Sun**, they have formed a close **conjunction**. Perhaps they were near one of the angles of the horoscope.

Ita Wegman's **birth** occurred just a few days before the **new moon**. We can see this in the proximity of the **Moon** to the **Sun**. At her **death**, the two 'lights' were also close to each other. Moreover, the **Moon** was near **Mercury** on both occasions.

Ita Wegman – Death on March 4, 1943 (12 noon ?)

---

[42] J. E. Zeylmans van Emmichoven, "Wer war Ita Wegman – 1876 – 1925 – Band 1" (Who Was Ita Wegman: A Documentation, Volume 1: 1876-1925), Verlag am Goetheanum, 3rd edition 2022, p. 64

Additionally, the **birth horoscope** shows an **opposition** between **Pluto** and **Jupiter**, which reappears as a **conjunction** in the **death horoscope**.

Mars, which at **birth** was near the **Ascendant** and close to **Pluto**, moved to an **opposition** with **Pluto** at her death. Again, the significance of oppositions and conjunctions, as well as their occasional interchange, is striking. The same is true for **Neptune** and **Venus**. In the **birth horoscope**, they are **near each other**; in the **death horoscope**, they are in **opposition**.

As in other horoscope comparisons, we also encounter in Ita Wegman's case the already frequently observed interchange between **Jupiter** and **Neptune**. At birth, **Pluto** and **Neptune** were below the Ascendant; at her **death**, **Pluto's** companion **Neptune** was replaced by **Jupiter**. Overall, a series of planetary connections from Ita Wegman's birth horoscope reappear in her **death horoscope**.

Albertus Magnus – Marie Steiner

Rudolf Steiner's closest and longest-standing companion was his later wife, Marie Steiner, née von Sivers. The two first met in November 1900 in Berlin, during the early phase of Rudolf Steiner's lecture activities. At that time, Marie von Sivers was 33 years old. From January 1902 onward, she tirelessly supported Rudolf Steiner in all developmental steps of the Anthroposophical Movement. This was her great life's task.

Anna Samweber, one of Rudolf Steiner's closest collaborators, provides insight into this relationship: *"Once, Marie Steiner (after Rudolf Steiner's death) showed me a letter from him in which he explained how it had been determined in the spiritual world that he could only fulfill his earthly mission together with her. This letter was among those very personal ones from Rudolf Steiner that Marie Steiner burned. When I asked her why she did so, as it was surely significant for the membership to know, she replied firmly: «I cannot possibly expose the most intimate matters to this society!»"* [43]

Years before her marriage to Rudolf Steiner, Marie von Sivers learned from him about her previous incarnation as the universal scholar (Doctor Universalis) and Dominican **Albertus Magnus** in the 13th century. His exact birth year is unknown, but he was likely born around 1200 near Lauingen on the Danube. Rudolf Steiner repeatedly endeavored to give his future wife an intellectual and spiritual access to her former incarnation. To this end, he always took her, during every visit to Cologne – even when they were in a hurry and often to Marie von Sivers' protest – directly from the main train station to the nearby St. Andrew's Church. Since the dissolution of the Cologne Dominican Monastery in 1804, the remains of Albertus Magnus have rested there in a Roman sarcophagus. At this site, he explained to her that in their last earthly life, she had been his teacher. In 1911 or 1912, a few years before their marriage, they were accompanied by *Helene Röchling* during one such visit to the sarcophagus of Albertus Magnus. She reported the following:

"After they had moved a few steps away from the sarcophagus of Albertus Magnus, Rudolf Steiner stopped and said with a smile – standing in a triangular formation – to Marie von Sivers: «Do you still remember the time of our work back then?» Marie von Sivers: «Only very vaguely.» Rudolf Steiner replied: «But back then, you were my teacher!»" [44]

---

[43] Anna Samweber, "Erinnerungen an Rudolf Steiner und Marie Steiner-von Sivers" (Memories of Rudolf Steiner and Marie Steiner-von Sivers), Verlag am Goetheanum, published by Jacob Streit, p. 39

[44] Ekkehard Meffert, "Mathilde Scholl und die Geburt der Anthroposophischen Gesellschaft 1912/13" (Mathilde Scholl and the Birth of the Anthroposophical

Albertus Magnus, the teacher of *Thomas Aquinas*, **died on November 15, 1280**, at an unknown hour in Cologne. Thus, we can create his **death horoscope**.

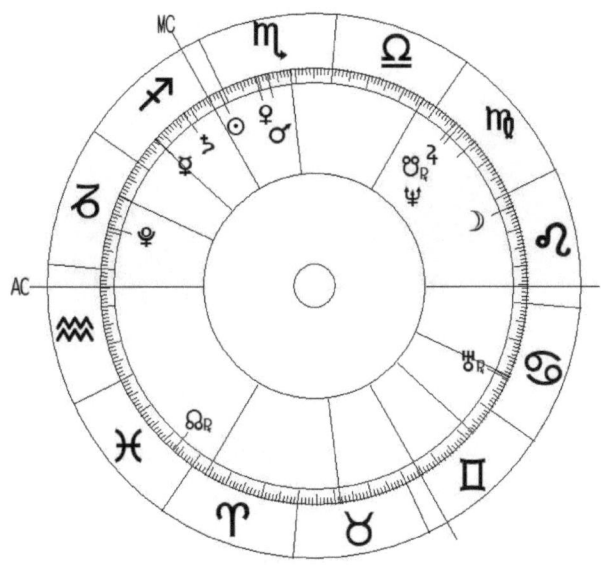

Albertus Magnus – Death on November 15, 1280 (12 noon ?)

Nearly six hundred years later, on **March 14, 1867**, Albertus Magnus was reborn as **Marie von Sivers** in Włocławek near Warsaw (then part of Russia). Comparing his **death horoscope** with her **birth horoscope** initially reveals two very different charts.

Society), Verlag am Goetheanum, p. 123 f. und p. 293, note 66; as well as Wilfried Hammacher, "Marie Steiner – Lebensspuren einer Individualität" (Marie Steiner – Traces of an Individuality), Verlag Freies Geistesleben, p. 245, note 24 with detailed information

Marie Steiner – Birth on March 14, 1867 (12 noon ?)

Upon closer examination, however, a recurring **conjunction** of **Neptune** with the **descending lunar node** becomes apparent, supported by **Jupiter**. At the **death** of **Albertus Magnus**, all three were in a close **conjunction**. At the **birth** of **Marie von Sivers**, this **conjunction** had widened somewhat but was still clearly visible. Its significant emphasis, in the manner observed in all previous analyses, came from proximity to one of the two 'lights'. On the day of **Albertus Magnus's death**, it was the **Moon**. At the **birth** of **Marie von Sivers**, it was the **Sun**. **Mercury** had taken the former position of **Jupiter** near **Neptune**, but **Jupiter** still remained nearby.

On **December 27, 1948, Marie Steiner passed away**. In her **death horoscope**, **Neptune** appears for the third time in **conjunction** with the **descending lunar node**. Once again, it is emphasized by the nearby **Moon**, as at the **death of Albertus Magnus**. **Jupiter** had moved very close to the **Sun**.

Marie Steiner – Death on December 27, 1948 (12 noon ?)

Mars was in **conjunction** with the **Sun** at the **deaths of both Albertus Magnus** and **Marie Steiner**. In the intervening **birth horoscope of Marie Steiner**, **Mars** appeared instead in **conjunction** with the **Moon**. Thus, we encounter once again the previously noted exchange between the **Sun** and the **Moon**, always aiming to emphasize certain planets or entire planetary groups.

Thomas Aquinas – Rudolf Steiner

Given the truly extraordinary individuality of Rudolf Steiner in so many respects, it is hardly surprising that he became aware of his previous incarnation at a young age. This occurred in the second half of his fourth seven-year period, after he had moved to Vienna, likely in the 5th year of this period.

In the current age, significant insights into our previous incarnations typically come from external sources—through comments from others who are often unaware of the significance of their words. Spiritual disciples may also receive internal hints from their personal angel, but external confirmation is always required.

"If you are to know anything about your previous incarnation, in our era you will not understand it from within yourself. Rather, your attention will be drawn to it through some outer event or through another person. In our time it is generally false when somebody looks within and then claims to have been this or that person. If we are to know anything, it will be told to us from outside." [45]

For Rudolf Steiner, this external hint came through a remark by the Cistercian priest Wilhelm Neumann:

"And then a noteworthy episode occurred. I was once giving a lecture in Vienna. The same person was there and after the lecture he made a remark which could only be interpreted in the sense that at this moment he had complete understanding of a certain man belonging to the present age and of the relation of this man to his earlier incarnation. And what the person said on that occasion about the connection between two earthly lives, was correct, was

---

[45]   GA 169 "Weltwesen und Ichheit" (Cosmic Being and the I), Berlin, lecture of 18 July 1916

not false. But he didn't understand that at all; it simply came from his lips." [46]

The decisive words for Rudolf Steiner were: *"The germ of this address, which you have given us to-day, lies already in Thomas Aquinas!"* [47]

Of course, this statement alone was not the sole basis for Rudolf Steiner's conviction of his prior incarnation. Over the course of his spiritual development, he acquired the ability to independently look back into his series of incarnations.

About his birth as the Dominican monk **Thomas Aquinas**, we know only that he began his new earthly life **shortly before or shortly after New Year's Day 1225** at Roccasecca Castle near Aquino in Italy. Unfortunately, we cannot create his birth chart due to the lack of an exact birth date. However, his **death** date is known: **March 7, 1274**, at Fossanova Monastery. The precise time is not recorded.

Regarding **Rudolf Steiner's date of birth**, reference is usually made to the information in his autobiography "My Life": *"I was born in Kraljevec[48] on February 27, 1861."* [49] However, an undated note from Steiner himself indicates a different date: *"My birth occurred on February 25, 1861. Two days later, I was baptized."* [50]

---

[46] GA 240 "Esoterische Betrachtungen karmischer Zusammenhänge – Band VI", (Karmic Relationships VI), Arnheim, lecture of 18 July 1924

[47] GA 74 "Die Philosophie des Thomas von Aquino" (The Philosophy of Thomas Aquinas), Dornach, Vortrag vom 24. Mai 1920.

[48] Donji Kraljevec, then Kingdom of Hungary, part of the Austrian Empire (now Croatia)

[49] GA 28 "Mein Lebensgang" (The Story of My Life), chapter I

[50] "Rudolf Steiner 1861 – 1925 – Eine Bildbiographie" (A Pictorial Biography), p. 16, Rudolf Steiner Verlag, 2021

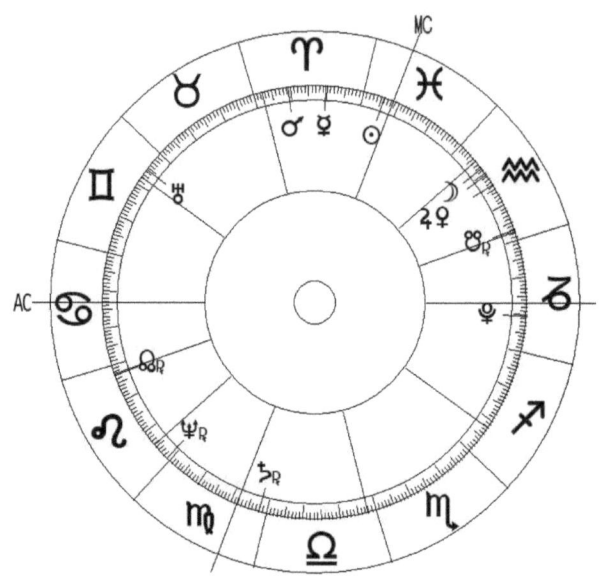

Thomas Aquinas – Death on March 7, 1274 (12 noon ?)

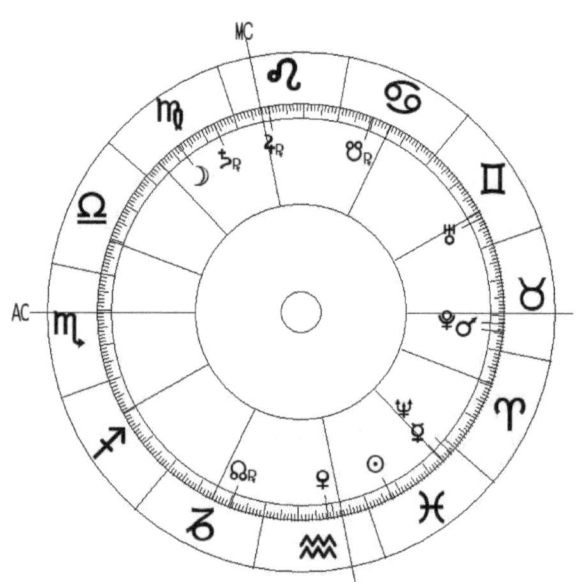

Rudolf Steiner – Birth on February 25, 1861 around 11:15 p.m.

All official documents list February 27, 1861, as his birth date. However, well into the 19th century, it was common practice to record the baptismal date as the official proof of birth. According to canon law, only a baptized person was recognized as an official earthly citizen. Anyone who has delved into genealogical research on their own family has likely encountered this fact multiple times. For creating Rudolf Steiner's **birth horoscope, February 25, 1861**, was used instead of February 27. The commonly accepted **birth time** is **11:15 p.m.**

Are there any similarities between the **death horoscope of Thomas Aquinas** and the **birth horoscope of Rudolf Steiner**?

Let's first look at the situation with the two 'lights.' In both charts we see **Saturn** is in **opposition** to the **Sun**, and in the same zodiac signs—Virgo and Pisces. However, due to the precession of the equinoxes, all planetary positions in ephemerides for Steiner's birth year must be adjusted by subtracting 6.25°.[51] This adjustment places five planets (Sun, Saturn, Pluto, Mars, and Uranus) at the transitional points between zodiac signs, underscoring the theme of transition.

For **Rudolf Steiner's birth horoscope**, the special feature results that not only the **Sun** and **Saturn** slip back almost at 0° Pisces and 0° Virgo, but also **Pluto** and **Mars** close to 0° Taurus, as well as **Uranus** almost at 0° Gemini. In total, five (!) planets are located in the transitional area between two zodiac signs. Doesn't this remind us of the local conditions during Rudolf Steiner's childhood? He grew up in the small town of Neudörfl, located on the border between Austria and Hungary, and had to cross the

---

51 See the table of correction values in the author's books "Influences of the Forces of the Zodiac on the Cultural Development of Mankind" (Fig. 6, p. 39) and "Ancient and Modern World View – Rudolf Steiner's Criticism of Astrology" (Fig. 4, p. 53), Publisher BoD (Books on Demand), Norderstedt

border river, Leitha, twice daily on his way to school and back home. This likely fostered within his soul the ability to establish balance between two polarities, which is the central principle of anthroposophy and the Christ impulse.

Furthermore, in **Thomas Aquinas' death chart**, the **Moon** is in **conjunction** with **Jupiter** and **Venus**, forming an **opposition** to **Neptune**. In **Steiner's birth chart**, this planetary group overlaps with the **Sun-Saturn opposition** mentioned above. **Jupiter** again appears close to the **Moon**, and **opposing** them, **Venus** and **Neptune**. Venus has simply moved to the opposite side of Neptune. This means that the group of four, the **Moon**, **Jupiter**, **Venus** and **Neptune**, remains intact. The latter has joined forces with **Mercury** and thus connects supernatural experience with the intellect.

On **March 30, 1925**, around **10 a.m.**, Rudolf Steiner laid down his earthly body in Dornach. In his **death horoscope**, we see **Venus** clearly moving closer to the **Sun**. The position where **Mercury** and **Neptune** were in **conjunction** at the time of his birth is now occupied by **Uranus**. This planet adds a new dimension to the **Sun-Venus conjunction**, and its proximity to the **Sun** significantly amplifies its influence. This particularity will be further discussed in the next chapter.

Furthermore, it is interesting to observe how the two **conjunctions** present in Rudolf Steiner's **birth horoscope, Saturn-Jupiter** and **Pluto-Mars**, are expressed in his **death horoscope**. The **Saturn-Jupiter conjunction** in the birth chart was accentuated both by its proximity to the **Moon** and by **Jupiter's** position at the **Midheaven**. In the **death horoscope**, this group appears in such a way that **Jupiter** and **Saturn** are positioned in the opposite quarter circle from the **Moon**, indeed far apart, yet the opposition point of the **Moon** is precisely in the middle (17° Sagittarius) between **Jupiter** and **Saturn**. This allows the **Moon** to act as a link not only between **Jupiter** and **Saturn** but also between **Mars** and **Pluto**, which were in a very close **conjunction** in the **birth chart** and received additional emphasis due to their position on the **Descendant**. Pluto has maintained its emphasis by shifting from the Descendant (at birth) to the Ascendant (at death). Such things can be assessed here, as both the exact birth time and the time of death are known.

Rudolf Steiner – Death on March 30, 1925 around 10 a.m.

We learn from this the diversity of variations that may occur in expressing the planetary characteristics of a **birth horoscope** in the subsequent **death horoscope**. The common aspect rules of both traditional and new astrology teachings are completely inadequate for this. They are far too narrowly defined.

Rudolf Steiner and the Masters of Esoteric Christianity

Rudolf Steiner was an extraordinarily gifted and versatile individual. He authored books and delivered lectures on a vast range of subjects, including education, philosophy, natural sciences, art, medicine, agriculture, spirituality, and more. His collected works comprise approximately 6,000 lectures in over 300 volumes. Even in 1924, following the fire that destroyed the first Goetheanum and despite beginning significant health challenges, Steiner delivered more than 400 lectures before his final address on September 28. This was possible only by giving multiple lectures on the same day. Simultaneously, he continued to establish the new School of Spiritual Science, engaged in countless conversations with members of the Anthroposophical Society seeking his guidance, worked on carving the wooden sculpture of the Representative of Humanity, and designed a model for the construction of the second Goetheanum.

For many, Rudolf Steiner was an incomprehensible phenomenon, not least because of his almost superhuman energy and creativity, as well as his unparalleled knowledge. Moreover, his extraordinary spiritual development, which allowed him to access higher realms of existence, made him not only a citizen of two worlds but brought him to the upper boundary of three: the physical, the soul, and the spiritual world—even reaching the higher Budhi plane, where the Bodhisattvas live in perpetual communion with Christ and receive from Him their missions for humanity's advancement. It is no wonder that, during his lifetime, anthroposophists speculated about the extraordinary individuality standing among them.

Understandably, these speculations took various forms. Some suggested Steiner was the **Bodhisattva Jeshu ben Pandira**, who lived among the Essenes a century before Christ and helped lay the groundwork for Christianity. Others came to the conviction that Rudolf Steiner was the great initiate **Zarathustra**, who was reborn as **Jesus of Nazareth**, surrendered his corporeality to the Christ being as an earthly shell at the Baptism in the Jordan River, and has since been contributing to the further evolution of humanity as **Master Jesus**. Others claimed that Steiner was an incarnation of **Christian Rosenkreutz**. Still, others speculated he was the **soul of the Nathan Jesus-child**, humanity's primordial soul from before the Fall. And even the opinion that he was the **Holy Spirit** was held by some anthroposophists after his death.

The question, "Who was Rudolf Steiner?" continues to occupy many people to this day, particularly those profoundly impressed by the uniqueness of his personality and work. Yet answering such a question involves significant risk. All too easily, this can give rise to a cult of personality, which could negatively impact the accomplished work of such an individual. Rudolf Steiner himself described the Rosicrucian path of initiation as the most appropriate for contemporary humanity. He was thus a member of the Rosicrucian movement. Around his neck he wore a pendant depicting the symbol of the Rose cross, a cross surrounded by seven roses. It was an artifact from earlier centuries, which he later bequeathed to Ita Wegman.

Within the Rosicrucian tradition, a strict law prohibits revealing the true individuality of one of its initiates until 100 years after their death, to prevent any cult of personality. Steiner explained: *"This has been a strict law within the Rosicrucian community since its foundation. Exoterically, no one knows who is a leader in the Rosicrucian community until one hundred years have passed after his death. Then what he has given has already passed over into humanity, has become the objective property of mankind. Thus everything personal is excluded. Never will it be possible to point to a personality in an earthly body as a carrier of the Christian mystery. Only a hundred years after the death of such a personality would this be possible. This is a law which all the brothers of the Rose-Cross well observe."* [52]

With the arrival of 2025, a century has passed since Rudolf Steiner's death. This means it is now permissible, within the boundaries of Rosicrucian law, to discuss publicly the mystery surrounding his person.

It is clear that Rudolf Steiner was not **Christian Rosenkreutz**. As early as 1904, in esoteric lessons connected to the Temple Legend, Rudolf Steiner disclosed that Christian Rosenkreutz had been *Hiram Abiff*, the great builder of Solomon's Temple, in a previous incarnation, and was reborn at the time of the Mystery of Golgotha as *Lazarus*, later becoming Christ's beloved disciple. [53] During that time, Rudolf Steiner, after his pre-Christian incarnation as *Aristotle*, was with *Alexander the Great* and other Michaelean souls in the solar sphere:

"Michael and his own, among them Alexander and Aristotle, did not experience the Mystery of Golgotha from the vantage-point of the earth; they did not witness the arrival of Christ on the earth, they witnessed His departure from the Sun." [54]

---

[52] GA 143 "Erfahrungen des Übersinnlichen – Die drei Wege der Seele zu Christus" (Experiences of the Supernatural – The Three Paths of the Soul to Christ), Stockholm, lecture of 17 April 1912

[53] GA 265 "Zur Geschichte und aus den Inhalten der erkenntniskultischen Abteilung der Esoterischen Schule – 1904 – 1914" (On the history and contents of the epistemological cult section of the Esoteric School – 1904–1914), appendix "Zur Hiram-Johannes-Forschung Rudolf Steiners" (On Rudolf Steiner's Hiram-Johannes research) by Hella Wiesberger, p. 423 ff.

[54] GA 240 "Esoterische Betrachtungen karmischer Zusammenhänge – Band VI", (Karmic Relationships VI), Torquay, lecture of 14 August 1924

Furthermore, **Christian Rosenkreutz** was one of two initiators of Rudolf Steiner. This is documented in *Friedrich Rittelmeyer's* account to *Walter Johannes Stein*, who recorded it in writing:

"Rittelmeyer states: When writing a biography of Dr. Steiner, Steiner, in the presence of Mrs. Steiner, shared that he had two initiators: Christian Rosenkreutz and Master Jesus (Zarathustra)." [55]

Thus, Rudolf Steiner could not have been identical with **Master Jesus (Zarathustra)**, as some claim.

Rittelmeyer provides additional context about Master Jesus, noting that he acted as the 'Gottesfreund vom Oberland' [Friend of God from the Highlands] in the 14th century, initiating the mystic *Johannes Tauler*:

*"Asked about the 'Gottesfreund vom Oberland', Steiner confirmed that he was **Master Jesus**, who has incarnated in every century since the Mystery of Golgotha. When asked if he was incarnated now, the answer was that Master Jesus was currently in the Carpathians, and Rudolf Steiner indicated he maintained a purely spiritual connection with him."* [56]

Rudolf Steiner was therefore neither Christian Rosenkreutz nor Master Jesus. But what about the speculation that Rudolf Steiner might have been the **Bodhisattva Jeshu ben Pandira**?

This too cannot be correct. When Rittelmeyer asked Rudolf Steiner in 1921 *"whether the Bodhisattva was already incarnated*

---

[55] Friedrich Rittelmeyer, "Meine Gespräche mit Rudolf Steiner" (My conversations with Rudolf Steiner), chapter "Die sieben Meister" (The seven masters), German Publisher Urachhaus

[56] Reported by Friedrich Rittelmeyer without any further indication of time. See GA 264 "Zur Geschichte und aus den Inhalten der ersten Abteilung der Esoterischen Schule (1904 - 1914)" (On the History and Contents of the First Section of the Esoteric School, 1904–1914), p. 238

on Earth", Steiner responded: *"If we live another 15 years, we may witness something of it. Those were his words."* [57]

Rittelmeyer later discussed this with Walter Johannes Stein. His notes from their conversation, preserved in the Goetheanum archives, confirm: *"Rittelmeyer says: In August 1921, Dr. Steiner spoke about Jeshu ben Pandira, saying that if we live another 15 years, we may witness something of it = 1936. Jeshu ben Pandira was born at the beginning of the century (Basel 1911)."* [58]

Rudolf Steiner was born in 1861 and had been publicly active in spreading Anthroposophy for twenty years by 1921. Therefore, it is impossible for him to have been the Bodhisattva Jeshu ben Pandira.

Could Rudolf Steiner have instead been an incarnation of the **soul of the Nathan Jesus child**? This soul was also present on Earth during the Mystery of Golgotha as part of the complex being of Jesus of Nazareth. Therefore, it is impossible for it to be identical to the individuality of Rudolf Steiner.

However, it is highly likely that in his astral body he carried a copy of the *soul of the Nathan Jesus*, in which the Christ-*I* lived for three years. As a divine being, as an avatar, Christ is capable of multiplying his etheric or astral body at will and integrating these copies into those individuals who have significant tasks to fulfill in the evolution of humanity.

The astral body contains the three soul components of a human being, and thus, over the past two millennia, *"the most diverse personalities had sentient soul, intellectual soul or consciousness*

---

[57] Friedrich Rittelmeyer, "Meine Gespräche mit Rudolf Steiner" (My conver-sations with Rudolf Steiner), chapter "Der Bodhisattva" (The Bodhisattva), German Publisher Urachhaus

[58] Ibidem

soul woven into them as copies of the astral body of Jesus of Nazareth." [59] The consciousness soul, in particular, is closely tied to the I. Accordingly, Rudolf Steiner explained in the same lecture:

"Among those who were more imbued with the copy of what had constituted the consciousness soul of Jesus of Nazareth, the special conviction arose, because the 'I' functions in the consciousness soul, that the Christ can be found in the 'I'. And because they had within them the element of the consciousness soul from the astral body of Jesus of Nazareth, the inner Christ rose resplendent in their souls. And through this astral body, they recognized that the Christ within them was indeed Christ Himself. These are the individuals whom you know as Meister Eckhart, Johannes Tauler and all the other bearers of medieval mysticism."

The threefold soul of Jesus of Nazareth was the soul of the Nathan Jesus child, into which the Christ-I later entered. All individuals who received copies of the astral body of Jesus of Nazareth thus bore an image of the soul of the Nathan Jesus child, and if it was specifically an image of his consciousness soul, also an image of the Christ-I.

*"From the 16th century onward begins the time when some individuals prepared themselves to receive into their I reflections of the Christ-I. One of these was **Christian Rosenkreutz**, the first Rosicrucian. It is thanks to this fact that a more intimate connection with Christ became possible, as esoteric teachings reveal to us."* [60]

We can thus assume that both Rudolf Steiner and a number of other disciples of Christian Rosenkreutz bore, or continue to bear, reflections of the Christ-I and the soul of the Nathan Jesus child within themselves.

---

[59] GA 109 "Das Prinzip der spirituellen Ökonomie im Zusammenhang mit Wiederverkörperungsfragen" (The Principle of Spiritual Economy in the Context of Reincarnation Issues), Berlin, lecture of 15 February 1909

[60] Ibidem, Rom, lecture of 28 March 1909

"In the case of a few individuals who were to be prophets for their own age, something was woven into their 'I'. Among them were the German mystics who proclaimed the inner Christ with such fervor because something like a copy of the I of Christ was embodied in them—only a copy or image of Christ's I, of course. Only human beings who prepare themselves gradually for a full understanding of the Christ and who will understand through their knowledge of the spiritual worlds what the Christ really is, as He surfaces time and again in ever changing forms during the course of human evolution—only those human beings will also gradually gain the maturity necessary to experience Christ in themselves. They will be ready to absorb, so to speak, the waiting replicas of the Christ-I, ready to absorb the I that the Christ imprinted in the body of Jesus.

Part of the inner mission of the universal stream of spirituality is to prepare human beings to become so mature in soul that an ever-increasing number of them will be able to absorb a copy of the I-Being of Christ Jesus."[61]

In the development of the new spiritual stream, **Christian Rosenkreutz** and **Master Jesus** work together intensively. On one hand, they incarnate in every century, unrecognized by their external surroundings; on the other hand, they speak through their disciples, particularly those whom they have personally initiated. Among these, as we already know, is Rudolf Steiner.

When a master speaks through a disciple, it usually occurs through a **temporary incorporation** into that disciple. This was particularly the case during Rudolf Steiner's lectures in the 'esoteric lessons' up until the First World War, as he himself hinted to his listeners, for example, on July 8, 1908, in Kassel:

---

[61] Ibidem, Munich, lecture of 7 March 1909

"The difference between exoteric and esoteric lessons: in exoteric lessons, the speaker assumes responsibility; in esoteric lessons, the being who is speaking through his mouth, the one standing behind him, assumes responsibility. We should regard the esoteric lessons as messages from such beings." [62]

Or on January 7, 1909, in Munich:

"It is necessary to always keep in mind that in an esoteric session, things are communicated to us directly from a supersensible world, and that the one speaking to us sees himself as an instrument used by the Masters of Wisdom and the Harmony of Feelings. Whoever listens to these communications with this understanding receives them in the right sense." [63]

Such temporary incorporations of beings into another human do not only occur between masters and ordinary people. It also happens that individuals from their existence between two incarnations temporarily 'incorporate' themselves into individuals on Earth. For instance, Rudolf Steiner mentioned this regarding the leading Platonists of the medieval School of Chartres:

"Up to now, these teachers of Chartres have not incarnated, although in my contact with the Cistercian Order I was able again and again to come across incorporations of many of those who were in the School of Chartres. In the Cistercian Order one met many a personality who was not a reincarnation of a pupil of Chartres but in whose life there were periods when—for hours, for days—he was inspired and penetrated by some such Individuality from the School of Chartres. It was a matter, in these cases, of incorporation, not incarnation." [64]

---

[62] GA 266 a "Aus den Inhalten der esoterischen Stunden – Band I" (From the Contents of Esoteric Classes – Vol. I), esoteric lesson of 4 July 1908 in Kassel

[63] Ibidem, esoteric lesson of 7 January 1909 in Kassel

[64] GA 240 "Esoterische Betrachtungen karmischer Zusammenhänge – Band VI" (Karmic Relationships VI), Arnheim, lecture of 18 July 1924

Are there, beyond this, also **permanent incorporations** that ultimately result in **dual beings**? Indeed, such cases exist, and one of the most well-known examples is Rudolf Steiner's wife, Marie Steiner. She was the permanent bearer not of a deceased human individuality, nor of a master of esoteric Christianity, but of a superhuman spiritual being from higher spheres. Rudolf Steiner therefore referred to his wife as a *"cosmic being."* When, during a lunch at Emil Molt's home, the conversation turned to Rudolf Steiner working on his autobiography *"Mein Lebensgang"* [65] and Emil Molt suggested, *"One should also write Frau Doctor's biography,"* Rudolf Steiner replied: *"That cannot be done. Frau Doctor is a cosmic being."* [66]

One could interpret this as a kind of compliment from Rudolf Steiner to his wife or as a poetic description of her nature. However, such superficiality was entirely foreign to Rudolf Steiner. As early as his first Mystery Drama, *"The Portal of Initiation,"* he gave a hint about the "cosmic being", whose bearer Marie Steiner was. In the drama, she played the role of Maria. Her spiritual teacher, Benedictus, the initiate, explains to her in the third scene:

"When in life's pilgrimage I had attained that rank which granted me the dignity to serve with counsel in the spirit-spheres, a godlike Being did draw nigh to me, who would descend into the realms of earth, and dwell there, veiled in form of flesh, as man. For just at this one turning-point of time the Karma of mankind made this demand. For each great step in world-development is only possible when gods do stoop to link themselves with human destiny. And this new spirit-sight that needs must grow and germinate

[65] GA 28 "The Story of My Life"

[66] Wilfried Hammacher, "Marie Steiner – Lebensspuren einer Individualität" (Marie Steiner – Traces of an Individuality), p. 139, German Publisher Freies Geistesleben,

henceforth in souls of men can only be unfolded when a god doth plant the seed within some human heart. My task it was to find that human soul which worthy seemed to take within itself the powerful Seed of God. I had to join the deed of heaven to some human lot. My spirit's eye then sought, and fell on thee." [67]

In the dramas, Rudolf Steiner even indicates the identity of this spiritual being: it was the wisdom-being long venerated in ancient mystery schools as "Sophia," who was also intimately connected with Mary, the mother of Jesus, standing at the cross. Rudolf Steiner linked Sophia and Marie Steiner in the drama by presenting the latter under the name "Sophia" in the prelude to *"The Portal of Initiation."* The wisdom-being Sophia had evolved into Anthroposophia. Marie Steiner was the bearer of this being, which explains Rudolf Steiner's constant need for her presence.

In the chapter "Albertus Magnus – Marie Steiner," a letter from Rudolf Steiner to her is quoted, in which he elaborates on *"how it had been determined in the spiritual world that he could only fulfill his earthly mission together with her."* [68] Furthermore, he was only able to begin his work in the spirit of anthroposophy after someone had asked him to do so, in accordance with an occult law. *Johanna Mücke*, the long-standing head of the Philosophical-Anthroposophical Publishing House, recounts a relevant conversation in which only she, Rudolf Steiner, and Marie Steiner were present:

"He explained that Frau Dr. Steiner had at the time asked him whether it wouldn't be possible to present these wisdoms in a manner more aligned with European intellectual life and with consideration of the Christ-impulse. [...] Herr Dr. Steiner added

---

[67] GA 14 "Vier Mysteriendramen" (Four Mystery Plays)

[68] Anna Samweber, "Erinnerungen an Rudolf Steiner und Marie Steiner-von Sivers" (Memories of Rudolf Steiner and Marie Steiner-von Sivers), Verlag am Goetheanum, published by Jacob Streit, p. 39

words that I will never forget: «With that, I was given the possibility to work in the way I had envisioned. The question was posed to me, and I could, according to spiritual laws, begin to answer such a question.» [69]

Marie Steiner possessed a very special etheric body that enabled her to be the bearer of the spiritual being Sophia/ Anthroposophia. This also predestined her to lead the new art form of eurythmy, through which the movements of the etheric body are made physically visible. The formative forces of the etheric body manifest physically in the principle of rounding. The principle of the straight line, of radius, originates instead from earthly forces. In Marie Steiner, the latter had to recede. Rudolf Steiner once described the consequence of this to *Roman Boos* as follows: *"You see, all her tips are too small—too small hands and feet, too small a nose. In this inwardness lies Frau Doktor's artistry."* [70]

Rudolf Steiner often desired Marie Steiner's immediate presence when working. It seems that she hosted a **permanent incorporation** of the spiritual being **Sophia/Anthroposophia**, which inspired him. Marie Steiner occasionally expressed frustration with her role as inspirer because it prevented her from working on her own writings in various locations. In February 1914, she wrote to *Mieta Waller* in Berlin:

"Now I must be an Inspiratrice, as the Doctor calls it, that is, a silent figure beside him while he creates." Or, *"I inspire until I become stiff."* [71] This reveals how essential Marie Steiner, as the

---

[69] Wilfried Hammacher, "Marie Steiner – Lebensspuren einer Individualität" (Marie Steiner – Traces of an Individuality), p. 135, German Publisher Freies Geistesleben,

[70] Ibidem, p. 141

[71] Ibidem

bearer of a permanently incorporated higher being, was to Rudolf Steiner's work.

If even his wife was a dual being, could it be that Rudolf Steiner himself also hosted a **permanent incorporation** of a higher spiritual being? Was Rudolf Steiner, too, a **dual being**? This would at least provide an explanation for his extraordinary abilities.

In fact, there are several indications that point in this direction. Of particular significance is a statement made by Rudolf Steiner himself, which formed part of a longer meditation instruction given to Ita Wegman and has fortunately been preserved in her estate. *Margarete Kirchner-Bockholt*, one of Ita Wegman's closest collaborators, recounts this:

"Regarding the second part of the [meditation] *verse, Rudolf Steiner stated that one should imagine oneself approaching the altar, dressed in a white garment. In front of the altar on the left is Christian Rosenkreuz, wearing the blue stole, on the right is Rudolf Steiner, wearing the red stole. This altar must be envisioned in the spiritual world. On another occasion, Rudolf Steiner remarked that in the spiritual world, both figures stand side by side, adorned with these stoles."* [72]

Through this meditation image given to Ita Wegman, Rudolf Steiner depicted himself as standing equally alongside Christian Rosenkreutz. This might initially appear as an extraordinary pretentiousness. After all, Christian Rosenkreutz, in his previous earthly life as Lazarus, was the beloved disciple of Christ who witnessed His death on the cross. He also served as the earthly vessel for a higher spiritual being, the individuality of *John the Baptist*, who had resided in the spiritual world since his

---

[72] Margarete und Erich Kirchner-Bockholt "Die Menschheitsaufgabe Rudolf Steiners und Ita Wegman Ita" (Rudolf Steiner's Mission and Ita Wegman), Private printing for members of the General Anthroposophical Society, Philosophisch-Anthroposophischer Verlag am Goetheanum, Dornach 1981, p. 98 f.

martyrdom. We know of this connection from Rudolf Steiner's "Last Address." [73] The **beloved disciple of Jesus** was a **dual being**, comprised of *Lazarus* as the bearer (later known as *Christian Rosenkreutz* from the Middle Ages onward) and the individuality of *John the Baptist*, who complemented *Lazarus* with the consciousness soul and the three spiritual members—Manas, Budhi, and Atma—forming a complete human entity.

If Rudolf Steiner, in his meditation instruction for Ita Wegman, positioned himself as equal to Christian Rosenkreutz, and we understand that any form of presumption was utterly foreign to Steiner, must we not then assume that he, too, was a dual being— namely, a bearer of another, highly developed spiritual being? What kind of being might this have been?

Once again, a look into the Mystery Plays provides further insight. Rudolf Steiner occasionally remarked that all the characters in the dramas were based on real individuals. As mentioned earlier, there is a connection between Marie Steiner and her dual roles as Sophia and Maria in the first Mystery Play. Rudolf Steiner himself further clarified the close relationship between both the characters in the drama and the real Marie Steiner by depicting the previous incarnation of Maria in the Middle Ages as a monk in a monastery.[74] This unmistakably points to **Albertus Magnus** as the previous incarnation of Marie Steiner.

One of Albertus Magnus's most notable real-life students was **Thomas Aquinas**. Rudolf Steiner drew a similar connection between Thomas and the character *Johannes* in the drama, the pupil of the abbot, by giving him the full name **Johannes Thomasius**. Moreover, Johannes Thomasius is depicted as the

---

[73] GA 238 "Esoterische Betrachtungen karmischer Zusammenhänge – Band IV" (Karmic Relationships IV), adress of 28 September 1924

[74] GA 14, second Mystery Play "Die Prüfung der Seele" (The Soul's Probation), 7th scene

companion of Maria, mirroring Rudolf Steiner's real-life relationship with Marie Steiner.

Some readers may argue that Rudolf Steiner is likely represented in the drama by *Benedictus*, the initiate and spiritual teacher of his disciples. Indeed, when Steiner was once asked how old one should imagine Benedictus to be, he promptly gave his own age. Thus, we find Rudolf Steiner represented in the drama by two figures: *Johannes Thomasius* and *Benedictus*. This dual representation hints at Steiner's own nature as a **dual being**.

If Rudolf Steiner was indeed the bearer of a higher spiritual being, akin to *Christian Rosenkreutz*—who, as Lazarus, was the bearer of the individuality of *John the Baptist*—then he would have been justified in giving Ita Wegman the meditation instruction in which he depicted himself as equal to *Christian Rosenkreutz*, standing before an altar in the spiritual world.

This immediately raises the question: for which higher being was Rudolf Steiner a vessel? Here again, the Mystery Plays offer clues. It is no coincidence that Steiner named one of his two representatives in the dramas **"Johannes."** The name carries profound significance. Steiner explained this in connection with the beloved disciple of Jesus, who later became the Evangelist:

"John had to develop to the point of Budhi in order to grasp what was revealed in Christ Jesus. The other three Evangelists were not so highly developed. John gives the highest, he was an awakened one. **John** *[German: Johannes] is the name given to all who are awakened. This is a* **generic name.***"* [75]

Did Rudolf Steiner, in the dramas, establish a direct link between the character *Johannes Thomasius*—a representation of himself—and the individuality of *John the Evangelist*, or even *John the Baptist*? In fact, he did so in at least two ways. First, the

---

[75] GA 94 "Kosmogonie" (Cosmogony), Munich, lecture of 28 October 1906

opening of the first Mystery Play features the figures of *Maria* and *Johannes*, precisely the names of the two most significant individuals who stood beneath the cross at Christ's death: **Maria** as the bearer of the spiritual being *Sophia*, and **Johannes** as the bearer of the individuality of *John the Baptist*.

Secondly, in the third scene of *The Portal of Initiation*, depicting Benedictus's meditation chamber, four portraits hang on the wall. They depict the last four incarnations of Benedictus's spiritual inspirer: *Elijah*, *John the Baptist*, *Raphael*, and *Novalis*. Since the character of *Benedictus* in the dramas also represents Rudolf Steiner, he thus established his own close connection to the individuality of *John the Baptist* in this way.

Steiner clearly understood, as early as 1910 when he began writing the Mystery Plays, the secret connection between *Lazarus* and the individuality of *John the Baptist*, even though he only partially revealed this to his audience 14 years later in his "Last Address." He had intended to share more details but was unable to do so due to his declining health.

In the first Mystery Drama, *The Portal of Initiation*, Steiner already established a similar connection to himself. He gave one of the figures representing him the name "**Johannes Thomasius**," linking it to his prior incarnation as Thomas Aquinas. He ended the name with "**us**," making it even more similar to "**Johannes Lazarus**." The parallel is unmistakable.

Thus, there are two bearers of the individuality of John the Baptist: **Christian Rosenkreutz**, formerly *Lazarus*, at the time of the Mystery of Golgotha, and **Rudolf Steiner** in the 20th century, formerly *Thomas Aquinas*.

From Margarete Kirchner-Bockholt's *"Additional Remarks on the Content of the Address of September 28, 1924,"* we learn of an additional explanation that Steiner gave to Ita Wegman regarding the dual nature of **Johannes Lazarus**:

"Lazarus could only develop fully from the earth's forces during this time up to the soul of mind and emotion [intellectual soul]; *the Mystery of Golgotha takes place in the fourth post-Atlantic period, and during this time the soul of mind or emotion was developed. Therefore, Manas, Buddhi and Atma had to be bestowed upon him by another cosmic entity, from the consciousness soul upwards."* [76] This occurred through the permanent incorporation of the individuality of John the Baptist, possibly even through a later exchange of the 'I.'

If we apply this to our current era of the consciousness soul, it suggests that Rudolf Steiner could only develop up to the consciousness soul through his own efforts. The higher spiritual members were supplemented by **John the Baptist**, who worked in service of the Holy Spirit or Paraclete. This also clarifies Marie Steiner's words, spoken about her husband years after his death: *"He was, indeed, the Paraclete."*

Two thousand years ago, **John the Baptist** was the herald of the physical Christ, and in the 20th century, he served as the herald of the etheric Christ. Rudolf Steiner alluded to this when he said in a lecture:

"Christ incarnated on the physical plane when humanity was confined to its physical body. **Today, we can repeat the words of the Gospel of John***: Change your mindset so that your faculties may open to the spiritual world. For people with etheric clairvoyance will behold Christ in an etheric body before them."* [77]

---

[76] GA 238 "Esoterische Betrachtungen karmischer Zusammenhänge – Band IV" (Karmic Relationships IV), "Additional Remarks" on the content of the address of 28 September 1924

[77] GA 118 "Das Ereignis der Christuserscheinung in der ätherischen Welt" (The Event of the Appearance of Christ in the Etheric World), Palermo, lecture of 18 April 1910

Here, the Baptist himself spoke. Since **John the Baptist** worked in and through **Rudolf Steiner** in lasting connection, we can now understand why Steiner named the planned predecessor of the first Goetheanum in Munich the "**Johannes-Bau**" (John's Building) and why the "**Johannesbau-Verein**" (John's Building Association) was founded to support its construction.

Furthermore, Rudolf Steiner's great joy becomes clear when Marie von Sivers was photographed in 1908/1909 standing before a bust of Novalis. Together, Novalis and Marie Steiner symbolized the remarkable collaboration between **John the Baptist** and the spiritual being **Anthropo-Sophia**, as well as their respective bearers, **Rudolf Steiner** and **Marie von Sivers**.

We have further information from Rudolf Steiner that the individuality of **John the Baptist** was the same that had been present in **Adam** when humanity's evolution on Earth first began. He described two Adam-souls that emerged from a common primal human soul. One part did not descend into earthly incarnation and thus remained untouched by the so-called Fall and original sin. Steiner called this part the *"Adam soul before the Fall,"* which had its first proper incarnation 2,000 years ago in the Nathan Jesus child of the Gospel of Luke. The second part of the primal human soul was the Adam soul that had already incarnated in ancient Lemuria as the earthly Adam and was endowed with the 'I' as its fourth member. Regarding this, Steiner explained:

"But the same 'I' that was withheld from the Jesus of the Gospel of St. Luke was bestowed upon the body of John the Baptist; thus the soul-being in Jesus of the Gospel of St. Luke and the 'I' in John the Baptist were inwardly related from the beginning." [78]

If the individuality of **John the Baptist** indeed worked in and through Rudolf Steiner, this means that the **individuality of**

---

[78]   GA 114 "Das Lukas-Evangelium" (The Gospel of St. Luke), Basel, lecture of 19 September 1909

Adam was active within him, as John the Baptist was merely a later incarnation of the same being. Who better to elucidate the significance of the human 'I' and the relationship between the two Adam-souls than Adam himself?

Did Rudolf Steiner ever express himself in this way to a trusted person? In fact, he did, in a conversation with *Anna Samweber*. In her biographical notes, she recounts a deeply moving and stirring conversation with Steiner following one of his lectures in Berlin:

"Afterwards, Rudolf Steiner spent time answering questions from members until nearly 12:30 a.m. When everyone had left, he came to me after midnight and said, «Sam, you wanted to ask me something, didn't you?» I had always tried not to burden the Doktor with personal questions, so I replied, «No, Herr Doktor.» But he insisted, «Yes, Sam, please ask your question!» Hesitantly, I said, «Well then, Herr Doktor, during the lecture, a question arose in me: Who are you? Who were you? Who will you be?» The Doktor immediately responded. He drew a curve on the table before me:

and said, «My individuality runs like a red thread through the entire evolution of the Earth and has existed even before its beginning.»" [79]

Who else could this description apply to but Adam? The individuality "Adam – Elijah – John the Baptist – Raphael – Novalis" is clearly of such a high order that it must be counted among the Masters. Remarkably, in his conversation with Anna

[79] Anna Samweber, "Erinnerungen an Rudolf Steiner und Marie Steiner-von Sivers" (Memories of Rudolf Steiner and Marie Steiner-von Sivers), Verlag am Goetheanum, published by Jacob Streit, p. 39

Samweber, Rudolf Steiner explicitly referred to **"his individuality."** This raises the question of whether Rudolf Steiner was not merely a **permanent incorporation** of the individuality of John the Baptist but may have experienced an exchange of the 'I,' requiring us to distinguish between the 'younger Rudolf Steiner' and the 'older Rudolf Steiner' in terms of the individuality dwelling within him. Regarding such a process, Steiner himself described the transition of the 'I' of Zarathustra from the Solomonic Jesus child to the Nathan Jesus child:

"Such a transposition of the 'I' also occurs in other cases; it is a phenomenon known to every occultist." [80]

When might such an exchange of 'I' have occurred in Steiner's life? One possibility is around the turn of the 19th to the 20th century, when he had passed his greatest trial and experienced his "standing spiritually before the Mystery of Golgotha":

"At the time when I made the statements concerning Christianity so opposed in literal content to later utterances, it was also true that the real content of Christianity was beginning germinally to unfold within me as an inner phenomenon. About the turn of the century the germ unfolded more and more. Before this turn of the century came this testing of the soul here described. The evolution of my soul rested upon the fact that I stood spiritually before the mystery of Golgotha in most inward, earnest celebration of insight." [81]

However, Steiner here speaks of a "germ" that unfolded over time. Perhaps, at this point, only a temporary incorporation of the Adam-Elijah-Baptist-Raphael-Novalis individuality occurred, similar to how other Masters temporarily worked through him during esoteric lessons.

---

[80] GA 114 "Das Lukas-Evangelium" (The Gospel of St. Luke), Basel, lecture of 19 September 1909

[81] GA 28 "Mein Lebensgang" (The Story of My Life), at the end of chapter XXVI

A later exchange of 'I' could have occurred after the first seven years of the 20th century, once Steiner had sufficiently acquainted his listeners with the foundations of Anthroposophy. This prepared the way for his spiritual Christology, particularly his Gospel lecture cycles. Significantly, Steiner began these cycles in 1908 with "**The Gospel of St. John**," [82] followed by the "**The Apocalypse of St. John**" [83] in the following month.

The 'later Rudolf Steiner' could thus be classified as an Adam-individuality among the ranks of the Masters. Is there a Master whose work spans the entirety of Earth's evolution as Adam's would? To a question posed by *Friedrich Rittelmeyer* regarding the Masters, Steiner once replied: *"There are two working in the East, two in the West, and two in the middle; **but one 'goes through'."*** [German original: "aber einer 'geht durch'."] [84] This likely means that this Master's influence encompasses all regions of the Earth and humanity as a whole. He has occasionally been referred to as "the seventh Master."

If the Adam-Baptist individuality was indeed present in Steiner, whether as a lasting incorporation or after an exchange of the 'I' even as a kind of incarnation, should this not also manifest in some way in **Rudolf Steiner's death horoscope**? Such a trans-formation in soul life would likely be reflected in a new planetary configuration—one that joins the typical constellations associated with the individuality of Thomas Aquinas–Rudolf Steiner as a kind of new influence. In fact, Steiner's death horoscope reveals a striking feature.

---

[82] GA 103

[83] GA 104

[84] Friedrich Rittelmeyer, "Meine Gespräche mit Rudolf Steiner" (My conversations with Rudolf Steiner), chapter "Die sieben Meister" (The seven masters), German Publisher Urachhaus

In examining the **horoscope of Raphael's death**, it had already become evident that the planet **Uranus** represents the karmic 'red thread' of this individuality—a planet whose orbital period of 12 x 7 = 84 years expresses the connection between the 12 zodiac forces and the 7 planets.

In the **birth and death horoscopes of Raphael and Novalis**, **Uranus** was consistently emphasized through its connection with one of the two 'lights'. At Raphael's birth, Uranus was in conjunction with the Moon (p. 70), and at his death, it was in conjunction with the Sun (p. 74). At Novalis' birth, Uranus was even in conjunction with both the Sun and the Moon (p. 74). At the death of Novalis, Uranus was linked with the Sun by opposition, with both being in conjunction with one of the lunar nodes— essentially representing the Moon (p. 76).

In **Rudolf Steiner's death horoscope** (p. 106), **Uranus** again appeared in conjunction with the Sun, even though it was not highlighted by conjunction or opposition with either of the two 'lights' in either the death horoscope of Thomas Aquinas or the birth horoscope of Rudolf Steiner. This signifies a new element in Rudolf Steiner's soul essence—one that cannot be derived from his previous incarnation.

Considering all this, must we not read Steiner's "Last Address" [85] with new eyes? Does it not lend a profound and additional significance to his comments on the incarnation sequence of *Adam – Elijah – Lazarus-John the Baptist – Raphael – Novalis*?

On September 28, 1924, Steiner already knew his earthly mission was nearing its end and that his strength for further lectures would soon fail. Does his "Last Address" not resonate like

---

[85] GA 238 "Esoterische Betrachtungen karmischer Zusammenhänge – Band IV" (Karmic Relationships IV), 28 September 1924

a farewell speech, implicitly asking Anthroposophists: "Do you still not understand who is speaking to you and who has been speaking to you all these years?"

They did not understand.

Thus, let these reflections conclude with the words Christ Himself once spoke to his disciples when they asked about Elijah, whom they had heard was to return. Christ replied:

"Elijah has already come,

but they did not recognize him."

(Matthew 17:12)

Afterword

As a supplement, the author would like to share a personal experience connected to the death horoscope of Rudolf Steiner. First, it should be mentioned that the author, even in his youth, encountered the phenomenon of being addressed not only externally but also internally. However, when he realized that his remarks about the "inner voice" were met with incomprehension by others, he decided to no longer speak of it.

In the summer of 2008, while finalizing the first draft of Part 1 of his treatise on the lemniscatory paths of the planets, something remarkable happened: he suddenly heard an inner voice saying, *"And now, check where **Uranus** was when **Rudolf Steiner died.**"* By then, such clear, internal messages were no longer unusual for him. However, as he was deeply immersed in completing the final sentences of his work, he found the interruption from this inner voice annoying. Moreover, his treatise contained no reference to Uranus, leaving him puzzled as to why this suggestion had arisen. Consequently, he replied internally, *"Not now! I need to finish writing first."*

Shortly thereafter, the same inner instruction repeated itself. Again, he dismissed it, feeling it was an unwelcome distraction while he was so close to completing his work. Once the writing was finished, however, the request came a third time. At that point, he decided to follow the prompt. He took the ephemeris and looked up the position of Uranus on March 30, 1925, the day of Rudolf Steiner's death. To his great astonishment, he discovered that Uranus was positioned in exactly the same degree of the zodiac—22° Pisces—as it was in the summer of 2008, after a full cycle through the zodiac.

The author realized that it was Rudolf Steiner himself who had made himself known and wished to convey that he had played an inspiring role in the writing of the treatise. This was likely also the reason why the inner message came precisely at the moment one might symbolically sign off on a completed work—much like a letter is concluded with the author's signature.

Those who lack personal experience with the "inner voice" might object, saying that Rudolf Steiner did not explicitly state, *"Look up where Uranus was when I died."* It is important to understand, however, that only deceased people whose physical voices one heard during their lifetime occasionally make themselves known with that same voice, so that they can be immediately recognized. For individuals whose voices one has never heard, the inner words are perceived without a personal tone. In such cases, if the speaker wishes to reveal their identity, they must provide their name. This, on the other hand, is something that adversarial beings can exploit by presenting themselves under false names. In the present case, this risk was irrelevant, as the instruction was simply to check the position of Uranus in the ephemeris for Steiner's death date.

This account exemplifies the typical way in which the masters communicate with their disciples. The masters' messages often connect directly to external events. This is particularly important in the early stages of a disciple's conscious connection with the masters, as it enables the disciple to discern whether what is heard internally originates from personal imagination or represents a genuine spiritual experience. Through such methods, the masters convey vital information to their students and occasionally issue them specific tasks—for instance, to write a book on a particular topic.

Spiritual disciples are also confronted with whisperings from adversarial beings at a very early stage so that they can practice developing their powers of discernment. Such experiences represent "trials of the soul" along the spiritual path, ultimately fostering strength and maturity. Rudolf Steiner vividly depicted such trials in his second mystery drama, *The Soul's Probation.*

In 2008, when the author experienced the event described above, he had not yet dealt in detail with the topic of the "death horoscope". However, the connection between **Uranus** and **Rudolf Steiner's death date** may well have been a form of preparation for this book written years later, as the masters always act with far-reaching foresight.

Roland Schrapp

Publisher:
BoD – Books on Demand,
Norderstedt (Germany)

Large format (DIN A4)
270 pages, 27 illustrations

Paperback (adhesive binding):
ISBN: 9783752690101

Hardcover (thread binding):
ISBN: 9783752602906

This book takes a completely new look at the Anthroposophical Soul Calendar. It is about the deeper meaning of the fifty-two weekly verses, which has remained essentially unexplored in the last hundred years since the first edition by Rudolf Steiner. A dense veil of Isis was spread over them, of which is well known that no mortal person can lift it. Only the immortal, psycho-spiritual human being, who knows himself at home in the extrasensory, higher worlds, is capable of doing this. Only to him the weekly verses reveal themselves as a travel guide through these worlds and lift him up to ever higher spiritual-cosmic realms until he reaches the experience of God, from where he gradually descends again into a new life on Earth, enriched in spirit and fertilized in his soul. If the reader embarks on this journey, the spiritual archetype of the Soul Calendar is ultimately unveiled to him and he achieves an extended understanding of Man and Christ. By many quotations from Rudolf Steiner's lectures and books, the author virtually lets Steiner himself elucidate the breathtaking depths of his mysterious weekly verses.

Roland Schrapp

Publisher:
BoD – Books on Demand,
Norderstedt (Germany)

Paperback:
178 pages, 18 illustrations

ISBN: 9783743124585

Between death and a new birth on earth, the human being lives through a long cosmic existence in the higher worlds. This is mirrored in the earthly life. Rudolf Steiner described its division into seven-year periods and the connection with the pre-birth existence in the planetary spheres. Apart from this, there is another division including higher spheres of the fixed stars. Rudolf Steiner only gave us a hint. In line whith this and based on his own experiences on the path of spirit discipleship, the author of this book gives examples how these different stages of life between death and rebirth can express themselves in the course of earthly life. He also explains in which of the seven-year periods the conditions for learning something about one's own previous incarnation are particularly favourable. In addition, he describes the connection of the later seven-year periods of earthly life with the Life Spirit (Budhi), as well as the preparation of mankind for receiving it by a development which Rudolf Steiner called the gradual "getting-younger" of mankind, and which started at the times of the primeval Semites in ancient Atlantis.

Roland Schrapp

Publisher:
BoD – Books on Demand
Norderstedt (Germany)

Paperback:
81 pages, 6 illustrations

ISBN: 9783755717072

This book is not a mere summary of Rudolf Steiner's statements on the connection of the forces of the zodiac with the ages, but it offers a whole new range of view points on astrology, astronomy and the cultural history of mankind. The author first describes the origin of the zodiacal images according to Rudolf Steiner's statements. Then he discusses why these images do not correspond either with the signs of the zodiac in traditional astrology or with the physically visible constellations of the stars, and what role the astronomy of the ancient Greeks plays in this. It is also explained why, when creating a horoscope, the planetary positions must not simply be taken over unchanged from the ephemerides. They need a correction due to the precession of the vernal equinox. This makes the book a "must have" for every astrologically interested person. Another topic is the varying duration of the ages and what questions this raises for modern astronomy. Finally, using the example of European cultural development over the last thousand years, it is shown that each age is divided into twelve smaller cultural periods, which in their characteristics correspond exactly to the series of the zodiacal forces. In this way it becomes understandable why the cultural development of mankind just happened the way it did.

Roland Schrapp

Publisher:
BoD – Books on Demand
Norderstedt (Germany)

100 pages, 9 illustrations

Paperback:
ISBN: 9783759742827

Rudolf Steiner was very critical of modern astrology in several lectures. He emphasized that true astrology can only be practiced in a higher state of consciousness. This leads to insights that are entirely in line with the world view of the planetary spheres, the zodiac and even higher levels of existence originally seen clairvoyantly by the people of ancient cultures. Over the millennia, however, this knowledge has fallen into decay. Today's astrology is no longer based on true concepts of the zodiac and the house system. This book describes the four stages of its decline and leads the reader back to its origins and true foundations.

The ancient spiritual world view with the angelic hierarchies is contrasted with the modern, spiritless astronomical world view. The reader also learns about the house system according to Rudolf Steiner. All of this makes it possible to understand both the great significance of the Egyptian Sphinx of Giza and the date set by Rudolf Steiner for the laying of the foundation stone for the first Goetheanum according to cosmological aspects.

Roland Schrapp

Publisher:
BoD – Books on Demand,
Norderstedt (Germany)

Paperback: 198 pages
Large format (DIN A4)
253 mostly coloured
illustrations

ISBN: 9783752604030

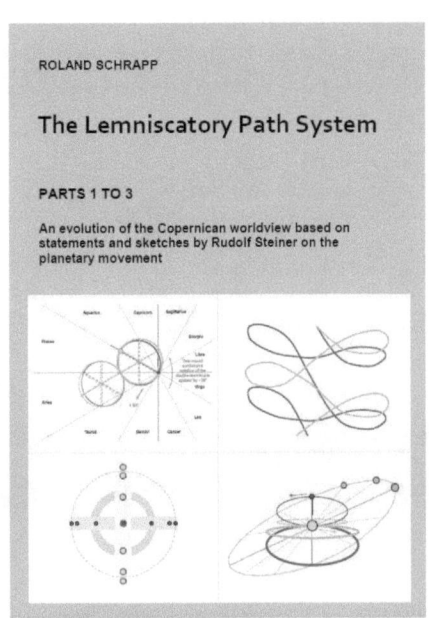

An evolution of the Copernican worldview based on statements and sketches by Rudolf Steiner on the planetary movement.

For the first time in almost a hundred years, Rudolf Steiner's statements and sketches on the subject of the "lemniscatory paths of the planets", distributed over several lecture cycles, have been brought into a larger context and examined for the consequences of this. Steiner's suggestions for a new consideration of the planetary movement were taken up and tried to develop them further in the given sense. The work "The Lemniscatory Path System" arose from this.

The treatise comprises 192 pages with 253 mostly coloured illustrations.